Praise for *What Are You Waiting For?*

"Beautifully raw, real, and courageous, Kristen Moeller shares her profound experience of a devastating fire and personal resurrection, showing us where we stop ourselves from living fully. In *What Are You Waiting For?*, you will get to know yourself, learn who you are when all is stripped away, discover your life's wild ride, and be drawn toward the pull of Grace. Enjoy this book!"

—Dr. Jennifer Howard,
author of the Gold Nautilus and Silver Benjamin Franklin
award-winning book, *Your Ultimate Life Plan*

"Kristen does so much more than just ask—she guides a reader to connect to the WHY behind all the waiting. It's a compelling invitation to move forward...at one or all levels."

—Mary Anne Radmacher,
author of *Lean Forward into Your Life*

D0067355

"Kristen Moeller's new book is full of inspiration and lessons hard-won. *What Are You Waiting For?* will help any reader explore their dreams, hopes, and fears so they can dive into life and fully embrace its messiness, its uncertainty, and its beauty."

—Kate Hopper,
author of *Ready for Air: A Journey through Premature Motherhood* and *Use Your Words: A Writing Guide for Mothers*

"As Kristen Moeller leads us through the devastating and life-altering experience of fire, she shows us how to rise from our own ashes to live life fully, powerfully, and authentically. *What Are You Waiting For?* will open and inspire you to live a life you love. A fantastic read."

—Sam Cawthorn,
author of *Bounce Forward:
How to Transform Crisis into Success*

"*What Are You Waiting For?* will give anyone an intimate view into genuine healing and growth. Kristen Moeller is a compassionate healer with an enormous gift for communication."

—Janet Attwood,
author of the *New York Times* bestseller *The Passion Test*

"All humans have the capacity to be resilient, whether it's during our darkest days or facing a simple life obstacle. Kristen Moeller's book, *What Are You Waiting For?*, helps us find that internal strength and lifts us above and beyond any anchor that may be holding us back."

—David Mezzapelle, author of *Contagious Optimism*

"I felt a deep sense of recognition reading this book about the universal quest to seek and search. Kristen Moeller shows us how to let go of questing and craving and embrace acceptance, which is the first step to a life of fulfillment and happiness."

—Nina Lesowitz, coauthor of *Living Life as a Thank You*

"*What Are You Waiting For?* is so much more than a gripping narrative and a how-to book; it lets you see you're not alone, and gives you permission to show up for your life right now, just as you are and just as you aren't."

—Kirsty Spraggon, author of *Work as If You Own It*

"What are you waiting for? Stop letting life pass you by! Kristen shows us how to stop waiting and start living NOW! Life is a moment-to-moment creation. Rather than waiting for the perfect moment, Kristen teaches us how to create them. *What Are You Waiting For?* will give you the tools to live an inspired, empowered, and fulfilling life now!"

—Laura Duksta,
author of the *New York Times* bestseller *I Love You More*

"Kristen Moeller has written a powerful guide for discovering the true meaning of trust. She invites us to release fear and open to the infinite possibilities of living fully."

—Cynthia James, author of *What Will Set You Free*

"*What Are You Waiting For?* is a powerful story of transformation under the most challenging of circumstances. Kristen will open your eyes to a whole new world of possibility and allow you to see your own life in a new way. Incredibly inspiring AND informative. It's a must-read."

—Bob Doyle, featured teacher in *The Secret*

"What Are You Waiting For? is a refreshing take on personal development where you can let go of the constant need for 'development' and find peace in knowing that where you are is exactly where you need to be. Kristen's stories are so brazenly honest that they touch you to the core and unveil the pieces of your life that you have been hiding from or neglecting to face. Reading this book, you will feel normal, connected, loved, and empowered to live an extraordinary life."

—Debra Berndt,
author of *Let Love In: Open Your Heart and Mind to Attract Your Ideal Partner*

"Kristen Moeller casts light on our ordinary perspective and makes a whole new perspective possible. By sharing her trials and errors, she embraces her extraordinary humanity and allows us to do the same. *What Are You Waiting For?* shows us our relentless and human journey of searching for an elusive destination when in fact we have already arrived. Kristen Moeller provides us with the one answer we forget was there all along. We have all the tools we need to build any life we desire."

—Kenneth L. Weiner, MD,
cofounder and Medical Director of the Eating Recovery Center

"I am so appreciative of Kristen's honesty and eye-opening journey to living now instead of in fear of what might be. *What Are You Waiting For?* is a question we should all ask ourselves and be brave enough to hear the answer!"

—Emme,
supermodel, television personality, and women's advocate

"Kristen Moeller reminds us of our forgotten dreams, goals, and visions we somehow abandoned in the process of 'getting it right.' With amazing clarity, authenticity, and love, Kristen leads us out of the limbo of seeking and waiting so we can become the architects of our lives."

—Clint Salter,
award-winning speaker, mentor, and consultant

"In *What Are You Waiting For?*, Kristen eloquently demonstrates how to become responsible for all areas of our life, including our relationship to money. So often, people don't get that wealth is a spiritual concept and that money is a byproduct of value creation. It's crucial to learn how to take responsibility for your life and do it in a way that is consistent with who you are from a spiritual perspective."

—Garrett B. Gunderson, author of *Killing Sacred Cows*

"Kristen Moeller is an amazing life coach who will radically change your life. Her book *What Are You Waiting For?* is full of wisdom, understanding, clarity, and practical action steps. As you read this book, you will remember that you are perfection right now. No need to wait to live your life; create your life right now! *What Are You Waiting For?* is a masterpiece!"

—Andrea Joy Cohen, MD,
bestselling author of *A Blessing in Disguise: 39 Life Lessons from Today's Greatest Teachers*

"Kristen Moeller's *What Are You Waiting For?* is a profoundly moving story. It is an exploration of loss and healing. It is a 200 plus page reminder to love ourselves however we are and to forgive ourselves for however we aren't. Reading this reminds me of the human spirit and its capacity for transformation. The book isn't just a memoir or a set of instructions but a skillful weaving of both. It carries you along her journey while inviting you to embrace your own. Where are you headed?

This is the tale of a woman, a fire, and a story that will bring you to tears and laughter. Kristen will spark the vision and actions you need to live powerfully and courageously."

—Shoshanna French,
owner of Simple Spirit: Intuition for the Real World

"*What Are You Waiting For?* delivers a heartfelt and inspiring message as well as a concrete action plan to get off the sidelines of your life and uncover your inner power. Kristen brings her nineteen years' experience in the field of personal development as well as her unique personal experience to provide readers a journey back to themselves—where they discover they don't have to 'wait for Jack,' or anything else for that matter, outside themselves."

—Pat Burns, author of *Grandparents Rock*

"Kristen Moeller nudges us out of our comfort zone and into the world of vibrant, unpredictable living. With deep compassion, wisdom, and wit, Kristen illuminates all the corners in which we hide so we can right ourselves, chin up and toes forward. *What Are You Waiting For?* will put you back on path with purpose and power."

—Martia Nelson,
author of *Coming Home: The Return to True Self*

"Kristen Moeller is a gift to us, a woman with a huge capacity to embrace our humanity. Having almost literally risen from the ashes of her own tragedy, she shares her hard-won wisdom, insight, and guidance to help us stop waiting and start living."

—Sharla Jacobs, Thrive Academy

WHAT
ARE YOU
WAITING
FR?

LEARN HOW TO RISE TO THE
OCCASION OF YOUR LIFE

BY

KRISTEN MOELLER, M.S.

FOREWORD BY JACK CANFIELD

V!va
EDITIONS

Published in the United States by Viva Editions, an imprint of Cleis Press, Inc., 2246 Sixth Street, Berkeley, California 94710.

Printed in the United States.
Cover design: Scott Idleman/Blink
Text design: Frank Wiedemann
First Edition.
10 9 8 7 6 5 4 3 2 1

Trade paper ISBN: 978-1-936740-52-9
E-book ISBN: 978-1-936740-61-1

Library of Congress Cataloging-in-Publication Data

Moeller, Kristen.
 What are you waiting for? : learn how to rise to the occasion of your life / by Kristen Moeller, MS. -- First edition.
    pages cm
 ISBN 978-1-936740-52-9 (pbk.)
 1. Self-realization. I. Title.
 BJ1470.M64 2013
 170'.44--dc23
                                    2013022403

To my best friend,
soul mate and husband, David—
with gratitude forever for your
undying support and love.
I am blessed to walk through
the fires of life with you at my side.

Life is a great big canvas, and you should throw all the paint on it you can.

—DANNY KAYE

Do I contradict myself? Very well, then I contradict myself, I am large, I contain multitudes.

—WALT WHITMAN

ACKNOWLEDGMENTS

Without the love and support of my friends and family, this book—and this journey—would not have been possible. Thank you all from the bottom of my heart to the tips of my toes.

Thank you also to my fabulous editors: Ellen Moore for keeping me going when all I wanted to do was stop, and for your brilliant contribution to these pages; this book would have remained "a good idea" without your guidance and love. Thank you to Kara Wuest at Viva Editions and Mary Ann Tate at the Art of Words for catching what I couldn't see. A book without an editor is like a peanut butter sandwich without the jelly—never complete, missing the sweetness, and hard to swallow. Thank you to the entire team at Viva Editions, especially to Brenda Knight for recognizing the gem in this book and being my champion as I walked through my fire.

CONTENTS

FOREWORD

It seems our dilemma as humans is to wait for an externally derived solution to our problems. We seem compulsive in our efforts to seek answers, comfort, and direction from "out there." We look to others for guidance and hope for a lightning bolt of understanding, expecting an authority outside ourselves—perhaps a book, a teacher like myself, or a spiritual belief—to tell us what to do and how to do it so we might finally be happy, healthy, and wealthy.

In this book, Kristen Moeller asks, "Why wait?"

With a wonderfully personal and engaging style, Kristen offers her intimate life story, providing a raw and powerful account of her personal struggles. With every chapter, she demonstrates her rare courage and willingness to be completely authentic while unflinchingly dismantling her life to see all the places where she has passively waited for something to change. She writes with the commitment to act, fiercely embracing her humanity so that the rest of us might do the same.

In each chapter, we have the opportunity to review our own journey, watch where we are stopped, where we are unresolved and stuck in our lives.

By the end of this book and your personal exploration, you

will see where you wait for life to begin. You will see that all the answers you need come from within. You will learn to stop hiding your magnificence—and you will learn to rise to the occasion of your life!

Jack Canfield
Coauthor of *Chicken Soup for the Soul®* and *The Success Principles*

PREFACE:
BURNING DOWN MY HOUSE

The time has come to turn your heart into a temple of fire.

—RUMI

Yesterday, I watched as the last of the metal scraps that once were my house were towed away. As the flatbed flexed to bear the load, I caught a final glimpse before it disappeared from view. Pieces of my home, bits of my life, memories turned into heaps of metal tumbled together, then vanished down the road on their journey to the recycling plant.

Three months into the year I declared "the year of letting go of attachments," my home and those of twenty others burned to the ground in a raging wildfire that turned lives upside down and killed three people. Had I known what would happen, I would never have uttered that declaration, yet most of us aren't given the gift of hindsight. What seemed like a promise to release my need to be more, do more, and have more turned into the biggest lesson in letting go that I'd ever had. Faced with tragedy, it's easy to ask "why?" During these times, it seems life does not make sense; it is not predictable, nor is it fair. We are confronted with the realization that anything can happen at any minute, that there are no guarantees. And then comes the choice: hang out in the angst of uncertainty, or simply accept life on life's terms.

Around the time of my declaration of letting go of attachments, I had said yes to the offer to write this book. After I'd dedicated my life to the theme of waiting while writing my first book, the topic had grown stale. I wasn't even sure what it meant any longer. Often, I pondered: What did it really mean to wait? What is the difference between waiting, patience, and procrastination? Was there any real hope that we might ever stop waiting? Were there appropriate times to wait instead of jumping? How could we possibly tell the difference?

We all have heard of deathbed regrets. We know we are supposed to seize the day. We see others selling out on their dreams—and we swear we wouldn't do that, yet deep down inside, we know we do. We wonder just how many second chances we need to be given. Just how many wake-up calls will it take for us to learn?

Like you, I have had my own share of wake-up calls during my short time around this rock. I recovered from severe addictions as a young adult; survived melanoma (thankfully we caught it early); lost pregnancies and people who were dear to me. And, each time something happens, I reevaluate life and believe that I gain a new perspective. Then, slowly, I slip quietly back into the status quo. In other words, I fall asleep at the wheel.

This is the tragic fate of the human condition. We have what might be called "spiritual narcolepsy." We forget who we are, what we are capable of, and what it is like to feel deeply, intensely, and joyously alive. We forget what it means to be free.

Here's the truth: Even before my house burned down, I wasn't free. I was waiting. If you had asked me, "For what?" I might not have known the answer. Yet there was a cloud of angst just beneath the surface, rearing its head from time to time to remind me of its presence. Even after a journey of personal growth spanning more than two decades, I longed to feel settled; I lacked the peace and sense of freedom I craved.

Seeing how I still waited rubbed me raw when I looked at it. One might think that, with a master's degree in counseling, a multitude of transformational programs, hundreds of self-help books, years of work with fabulous mentors and coaches, I would be at peace. Yet my drive for perfection wormed its way into my quest for growth, shrouded in the cloak of personal development. I deceived myself into believing that, with enough study and practice, I would be "fixed." I would arrive. I would attain the elusive state of perfection. I would find meaning, perhaps even the meaning of life! And *then* (and only then) would I be free.

But the more I searched for the "answer," the more I missed the point.

Had my house not burned to the ground, this would have been a very different book. I might have played it safe. I might have hoped to give you the "Five Simple Steps To Never Wait Again!" But guess what. There are no "Five Simple Steps." *They don't exist.* There is no "quick fix." So, instead of my watered-down words on waiting, while I continued to wait my life away, you are getting a fresh take, a heightened sense of urgency, and an increased compassion for our human struggles.

In the transitory period after I lost my home and all my possessions, grief became my teacher. While struggling to live a still-vibrant life, I developed a whole new respect for both jumping into action and what it means to wait. I learned the true difference between waiting as a way of avoidance and malcontent and the type of patient, allowing waiting required for going through a grieving process. As I peered deeply into my old behaviors, I began to relax my grip on the idea that life would go the way I thought it should.

Where once I had celebrated my intense push to succeed, that now felt as barren as the smoldering remains of my home. Instead of my driven-ness, what began to emerge as the smoke cleared and the ashes settled was a new-found freedom to simply be.

And yet if, once and for all, I could tell you the secret to waiting—the mysterious reason for why we wait and how to stop—I just might be tempted. For so long, I wished for a magic wand to wave and make this whole crazy world make sense. Now, I don't believe that wand exists. Instead of a wand, I will offer words and tales for us to discover together the very things that keep us stuck in life, and keep us waiting to feel free.

I will walk with you, to shine a light, illuminating the nooks and crannies of life where waiting hides out. We will dive in and explore lost dreams and forgotten goals. We will discover our deep-seated reasons behind the waiting. We will turn away from quick fixes that soothe us temporarily but leave us wanting more. We will tell the truth about all the ways we wait in life and come to terms with the impact waiting has had in the past, how it robs us even now, and how it will continue to rob us in the future if we don't alter our path.

The truth is, you will wait again. We won't pretend this isn't so. We won't slap on a bandage and take empty actions that stem from our attempts to deny this fact. Life doesn't come wrapped in a neat little package—yet so many of us seek just that. And, when it doesn't turn out that way, we are back where we started, wondering how we got here *again*.

While writing this book I lived in friends' basements, in hotel rooms, for a short while in a 1967 Airstream trailer on our burned-out land, then finally in a new home in a different setting. As I wandered, I wondered. As I wondered, I wrote.

In these pages, I am sounding the fire alarm. I am calling out the troops. I am shouting from the rooftops: "It's time to wake up!" And I am whispering in the dark. I am calling you gently. I am encouraging you to inquire into what begs for your attention. As you read my words, I hope to assure you that I understand the struggle, while reminding you of what you are here for.

This journey is not for the faint of heart. Peering into the depths of our souls to see the truth is for the brave. Continuing to catch ourselves when we wait again with compassion and a gentle spirit is the way of the lion-hearted.

INTRODUCTION:
WHAT THE HECK ARE WE WAITING FOR?

> *Everyone is just waiting.*
> *Waiting for the fish to bite*
> *or waiting for the wind to fly a kite*
> *or waiting around for Friday night...*
> —DR. SEUSS, *OH, THE PLACES YOU'LL GO!*

It has been said the journey within is the most important journey of all. Many of us follow a path, searching for meaning—for something "bigger." A lot of us have been doing this for a very long time. We have the skills, we have the know-how; we are wise beyond our years and generous to a fault. We have attended a legion of trainings, workshops, and retreats. We have studied with the teachers, masters, and gurus. We may even have become a teacher, master, or guru ourselves. With this level of dedication, you would think we would be happy.

Mostly we are. Then there is that small, vexing voice that keeps us craving what we don't have, desiring things to be different, and hoping one day to arrive at some magical destination just on the other side of the horizon. We don't *quite* let ourselves rest in who we are or where we are. Instead we continue to seek and search. And all the while, we wait.

Once upon a time, we simply waited for the basics. We waited to earn more money, to have less debt, to get married (or to get divorced), to have children, to retire. Many of us even waited to become spiritually enlightened! We hoped the next new experience or seminar or retreat would give us the answer. We waited for the right teacher to say the right words and hoped all would fall into place. We waited for recognition, to be discovered, to feel safe, to get it right. We waited to feel inspired (one of my personal favorites). We waited until our affairs were in order, our eggs in different baskets, our ducks in a row. We waited for world peace or the next president or a new car. Some of us even waited to die.

We live in interesting times, and, as the world continues to change, the waiting game changes too. These days we are busier than ever before. We are clearer about our purpose and why we are here, yet we often sense that something is still amiss. As the earth seems to spin faster and faster on its axis, a craving emerges from down deep, turning into an itch we can't quite scratch. We look around at all the change, transformation, and upheaval that surround us and, even though we marvel, we find that in our heart of hearts what we really want are some old-fashioned guarantees. We want this wild and wacky world to make sense and even to slow down for just a moment so we can catch our breath. We keep searching for that magic pill—the one that would make us, the world, and everything all right.

And, at this rate, we could wait forever and ever *and ever.* This crisis may be subtle, in that our waiting might slowly fizzle the life force right out of us, or it might be severe, where we one day wake up and realize it's too darn late. That's the thing about waiting—it is inherently sneaky. It *seems* so eminently reasonable, like the right or wise thing to do, given our current precarious state. Then it takes over as a quiet, often unconscious decision that traps us in its murky depths.

The result of all this waiting is that we have lost our freedom to simply be. And, when I say "be," I mean that deep-down, knowing sense of who we are and what we are made of, that quiet peaceful voice that tells us we are OK, the ease of feeling at home in our own skin. Instead, we have false images of *how* we should be, *who* we should be, *what* we should be, and, most of the time, in our own estimation, we don't come anywhere close.

The time has come to stop waiting for the world to make sense. The time has come to stop waiting for life to slow down and things to settle out. The time has come to live our lives anyway—in the face of waiting, of massive upheaval, as well as everyday stumbling blocks. If this really is (and I will borrow the profound words of Mary Oliver) our "one wild precious life," what are we doing about that? Will we live in fear of the other shoe dropping, the bottom falling out, or the house burning down? Or will we go forth anyway, into the unknown, embracing the uncertain and reveling in the wildness of the in-between?

That's what it means to stop waiting. It means we go forth anyway. We go forth into our dreams, hopes, and fears. We live that dream we have tucked away for a rainy day. We take that leap we have always hoped to take even when we don't know how it will turn out. We simply come to know ourselves as people who go forth anyway, people who keep moving when all we want to do is quit, people who fall to our knees and get up, time and time again.

We also come to know when stopping is the kindest thing we can do for ourselves, and we learn patience for our souls in a way we have never experienced before.

This is what real freedom is, to be at peace with ourselves, even in the face of all fears and hopes, even in the unknown while we confront the seductive pull of waiting.

It's time we wake up—and maybe we don't need an emergency—to remind us of this fact. Maybe, a gentle knock is enough.

The tragedy of life is not that it ends so soon,
but that we wait so long to begin it.
—W.M. LEWIS

The book is about the concept of waiting. It's about noticing the waiting and waking up to its effects. If you're a human being, you'll probably fall asleep again, but you can wake up a little quicker each time once you know what waiting looks and feels like for you.

You will have the opportunity to distinguish how, where, why, and for whom you wait, and you will discover some ways to get moving again. However, we are not talking about diving into frenetic frenzied activity in every area of your life. True, some people like more movement and activity than others, but this "carpe diem" nonsense, if taken too far, just leads to burnout. We will celebrate seizing the say, and also celebrate just hanging out with the day and maybe watching some sunsets or dogs or Netflix.

You will clarify what matters to you. You will hopefully let go of some of the waiting that doesn't serve you—the waiting that gets in the way of living—and embrace more of the waiting that is actually patience, acceptance, allowing, transforming—gently and all in good time.

By the end, you can discover who you are, what you really want and who you want to be when what is unessential is stripped away.

In each chapter, we will be looking at a different type of waiting. You will be distinguishing some of the ways you'll know it's there, where it's hiding, and where it might scuttle off to hide next. You will also receive some suggestions and practices to deal with waiting and some ways to move through, into, or around it that both the gigantic Soul You and the smaller Everyday You can learn to live with.

Perhaps once we are cleared of some old holding patterns, we really can greet our life with a "Hurrah!" instead of the fear that so often grips us, trips us up, or stops us cold. Perhaps we can finally accept that nothing is certain, that to be human is to be messy, and that throughout it all, we don't have to wait for life to be ironed out. Perhaps then we will experience the freedom we have waited for all our lives.

Imagine this:

You come to the edge of a cliff. You look down and wonder. Once you might have jumped, but now you play it safe. Deep down, you know who you really are and why you are here. You crave freedom—freedom to be and to do and to discover yourself. You feel called to make a profound difference in the world. You feel the pull of internal peace. Yet, you linger on the edge, unsure of what to do next.

Now ask yourself: Where did you lose your freedom to fly?

Chapter 1:

Waiting for Me

Age has given me what I was looking for my entire life—it gave me me. It provided me the time and experience and failures and triumphs and friends who helped me step into the shape that had been waiting for me all my life.

—MOLLY IVINS

Perhaps you are curious as to how one becomes a Professional Expert on Waiting. I am not sure whether we are born, or made, or both, but it feels like an arena in which I've had exceptional talent for a long, long time.

I don't remember when I first became a seeker. It may have been during the time spent in my mother's womb, as I sought a way out while I impatiently waited to be born. Or perhaps I emerged thinking I was in the wrong place—that back in "there" was better than "out here" in the world. For as long as I can recall, I have felt a longing for something else coupled with a chronic dissatisfaction with wherever I am. What began as a quiet (if unnerving) companion snowballed into full-fledged addiction as I sought anything and everything to take me away from me. Much later, after years of recovery, I discovered that my desire to seek was a clever cover-up, hiding the chronic dissatisfaction that remained.

To be clear, there is nothing inherently wrong with being a seeker. A lot of seeking is our answer to life's call that we grow into our most interesting, expansive selves. Many of us wouldn't be where we are today if we hadn't taken this journey. Additionally, it's a fact that most people who are drawn to personal growth are pretty darn cool.

The "problem" lies in our insatiable quest to be somewhere other than where we are right now, or to be someone other than who we are right now. It is our yearning to "arrive" at a future destination that somehow holds our happiness permanently at bay. Putting it bluntly, we are bottoming out while our life burns by.

On September 25, 1989, on a profound level, I stopped

waiting—and started arriving. After seven long and brutal years of struggling with bulimia, alcohol, and drug addiction I leapt into the unknown by saying yes to a life of recovery and began my journey to myself.

I would love to say that I never waited again, but as I have already shared, that wouldn't be true. The sad little girl that I was is long ago and far away. Yet I have compassion for her as even today, over two decades later, I can still remember the darkness of her alienation, confusion, and despair. And what I have come to understand is that some of the darkness remains, often lying dormant, then springing to life in times of stress, lurking patiently and waiting for a vulnerable moment. At other times, it's simply there as a quiet whisper attempting to catch my attention and take me off course. Much of my path of recovery has been about coming to terms with this fact.

My life today looks nothing like that half-life of compromise, degradation, and rigid constraint that is the life of an addict, yet all of that pain helped to make me who I am. I did not transcend the struggles of the human condition. I merely learned I can walk though struggles—sometimes with grace, and other times crawling through the muck, deep in the trenches, wondering if I would ever make it through.

Our challenges can make us into stronger and perhaps more interesting people. Yet in these interesting times, we are not exactly celebrating. We are not usually saying, "Whooohooo! My struggles are fabulous! I will have new depth and maybe even be super-cool." No, we are saying, "Ouch, I don't want this." Or, "Why me?" Or even, "What problem? I don't see any problems!" We are trapped on the metaphorical rails of our own pain and resistance as the train rushes toward us.

Without my struggles, I would not have the compassion I have today. I would not have chosen the line of work I did. I would not be where I am in my purpose, passion, or perspective. I was one of the lucky ones—to begin with, I made it out of addiction. The truth is that most don't. Some die. Some return headlong into the obsession, or transfer their obsession into other dangerous substances, ideas, or relationships. Some dabble with recovery for the rest of their lives, never quite getting there, forever waiting. I was miserable enough—and after two treatment centers I was blessed with willingness. A willingness to do what it took to recover. A willingness to put my trust in my treatment providers. A willingness to do what was suggested. And, perhaps most essentially, a willingness to have life be different than it was.

> The gift of willingness is an essential component to our exploration of waiting. With willingness, we can put one foot in front of the other even in times of great darkness. In doing so, we learn to trust ourselves. The nice thing about willingness is that you don't have to wait until you *feel like* being ready to do something. No great inspiration is required. Willingness is simply an opening, an agreement with yourself to do your best regardless of your habitual feelings.

When I think about those early days, the memories come flooding back. The embarrassment, the hopelessness, the lying, the manipulation, the fear, the disgust all kept me trapped, telling me their lies, begging me to give up and let myself sink into their murky depths. In my later years as a therapist working in treatment centers, I saw all versions of people stuck in the cycle of addiction, waiting to recover. I would see the light come on in a patient's eyes and sometimes it would continue to burn brightly. For others it would flatten and go dull, and my heart would sink. I knew that true recovery was possible. Yet over and over I watched people return to their disease. I recognized their struggle, I felt their pain as I attempted to reach into their hearts and let them know there was another way.

Throughout my years of addiction, I never knew there

was "another way" either. In my early days of recovery, I was only scratching the surface of beginning to understand why I struggled. Only much later would I come to understand more clearly what led to my sensitivity in the first place.

My world was first rocked when my parents announced their divorce, seemingly out of the blue. Thinking I must be at fault in some way, I decided from then on that I would be good, I would get it right, I would be a perfect little girl. I would find a way, somehow, to achieve a perfection that would protect me and my family from any more pain or chaos. Yet for some strange reason, no matter how hard I tried, I seemed to mess it up.

Another crushing blow to my already oversensitive soul was in the third grade when my class read aloud. As I waited for my turn to read (which always seemed to come too soon), my heart beat faster. I began enthusiastically, but faltered at the point in the book where it said, "Chicago is known as the Windy City." *What is that unfamiliar word? How do you pronounce it?* I floundered. Plowing onward, I said, *"Chick-*a-go is known..." Before I could finish the sentence, the entire room (it seemed) erupted in laughter. My face burning, I sank into my chair in complete humiliation. At that moment I made another critical decision: I never wanted to feel that way again! Therefore, I would never again speak in class without positively *knowing* the answer. This embarrassment was so extreme that for the remainder of my school career I would remain silent, even if

I *was* certain I knew the answer. What if I was certain but I was wrong despite my certainty? This strangling worry and constrained behavior followed me throughout my life, even in graduate school where I earned straight A's.

Around age nine, I was in love with horses, and was gifted with riding lessons. This was all well and good until I realized I needed to perform in front of others. One morning we were to practice jumping, and I learned people would be *watching*. Instantly, my stomach turned in knots. As we drove to the stable, I watched the familiar scenery pass by the window, my fear gripping me tighter and tighter as we approached. "How can I get out of this?" I silently asked. If my mom was driving, I could pretend to be sick and she would let me off the hook, but this time it was a friend's mom behind the wheel. Sinking into my seat, I bargained in silence: "There must be something I can do."

As we trotted our horses to warm them up, a seemingly brilliant plan popped into my mind as I stared longingly at the ground. I would fall off my horse and pretend to hurt myself. Once I was hurt, they couldn't force me to ride. And, most importantly, I would not be judged by the onlookers. As I slid off the saddle, aimed at the ground, another piece of my future came into formation. The danger of scrutiny turned to sympathy. Eureka! Hurting myself, I realized, was not only a way to get attention, but it was a way out of things I was afraid to do.

What began innocently enough became a way of life. In high school, to fit in, I turned to drugs and alcohol. By my junior year in high school, I was having "liquid lunches" with my friends as we slammed bottles of cheap wine while racing back to school before the bell rang. On other days my boyfriend and I ducked into his Trans-Am to do lines of cocaine. Somewhere during this time, I made the irrational decision that I needed to go on a diet. After throwing up for three days with the flu, exhausted and dehydrated, I stepped on the scale. "Look at that! Five pounds magically disappeared!" I thought, and another part of my future fell into place.

I began vomiting my food whenever I felt slightly uncomfortable with what I had eaten. I believed I could handle it, but it wasn't long before I realized *it* had *me*. I couldn't stop. I grew increasingly frail and thin. Even I eventually noticed. My concerned boyfriend lovingly fed me my favorite foods to help me grow stronger. I reveled in the attention, yet couldn't stop my downward spiral.

I moved to Boulder, Colorado, to attend college. Even with my gaunt frame and strange eating habits, I successfully managed to hide my eating disorder from everyone who knew me. There was no need to hide my alcohol and drug use. It seemed everyone liked to party, and there were *many* parties. After the local bars closed for the night we'd either stay up for hours snorting lines of coke, or I would sneak off to binge and vomit. I'd find an excuse to ditch my friends, and I'd drive around aimlessly in the dark, bingeing, then finding a safe place to purge.

The emptiness I felt was extreme—like a black hole that continually sucked the life out of me. Yet still, on the surface, I appeared to be a normal college girl. I constantly compared my insides to others' outsides and came up short. Not pretty enough, smart enough, popular enough. My nose was too big, lips too small, legs too short... The list went on. If I couldn't be as pretty as the other girls I compared myself to, I could at least strive to be thinner. Since college is often a breeding ground for eating disorders, being the thinnest was an uphill battle. I was socially awkward, comfortable only with my best friends or when I was drinking and doing drugs, which during this part of my journey was on a regular basis.

I was able to keep my eating disorder a secret for years, yet one afternoon while driving home from one of my rare sanctuaries, the tanning bed, I smoked a joint. When I got out of the car I felt odd. Stumbling up the stairs to my room, I opened the door, my eyes rolled back into my head, and I collapsed with a seizure. Observing this event, my alarmed roommate called for help—and called my parents.

Without the intervention of my parents, I would not have started my recovery at such a young age, and who knows where I might be today. I am eternally grateful that they were willing to confront my behavior. They educated themselves, talked to experts, read books, researched treatment centers, and were involved throughout my treatment process. Even though they were divorced at the time, they put their differences aside and united in the efforts to get me the help I needed.

However, I was the one who ultimately had to say yes to a new way of life—and stop waiting. I had to start choosing some health and happiness *now*! It was time to stop waiting to be perfect, waiting to be lovable, waiting to be OK. Saying yes at that moment was when I actually started to grow up.

Those with eating disorders have to deal with and ultimately make peace with the fact that eating is essential for healthy living; it took me a long time to be comfortable with food. After putting my trust in my counselors, I slowly learned to trust myself and then to trust the food. I began to see that three meals a day wouldn't make me "fat"—which for so long, seemed to be my greatest fear. I now recognize that it was a surface fear covering up all the anxiety that can go along with being human and all those feelings I was afraid to face.

A life of addiction is the ultimate in waiting and an example of the extremes of the human condition. Addicts often spend years (or a lifetime) caught in the cycle of addiction, waiting for that one day where it might become suddenly easier to stop than to continue. That moment doesn't usually come until the pain is great enough, and until then an addict stays in an infinite holding pattern with the repeated illusion that things will get better someday. Addicts or not, we can learn from this behavior. It's like looking at the concept of waiting under a microscope. We get to clearly see the pitfalls and pitifulness of a life on hold.

As a therapist, I observed parents attempting to come to terms in different ways with their child's illness. It is heartbreaking to watch one's child (whether grown or young) struggle with an eating disorder. So often, friends and family members ask me my advice for having their loved one choose recovery. Sadly, there is no easy answer. There are no magic words. But that doesn't mean we can't do anything.

Finally, after two treatment centers, I was ready to start at square one. Without the grip of addiction, I had a new baseline from which to begin. No longer just surviving, I learned what it was to thrive, and for a while this was more than enough. Yet as the years passed I saw something missing for me, as well as in the eyes of my friends, my loved ones, and even people I passed on the street. What was this faraway look? What was missing for so many of us? It seemed that, even with lives full of family, friends, careers we enjoyed, and a sense of purpose, we were still dying with our music still inside us. We were waiting for *something*.

In 2008, I threw myself into the topic of waiting with a vengeance. I wrote the predecessor to this book and launched a radio show called "What Are You Waiting For?" where I had the good fortune to interview many experts and laypeople alike on what it meant to wait, why we continued to do so, and how to stop. For years, I was engrossed in this endeavor, yet, even with all the knowledge gained along the way, as I have already shared, I still waited—and the sad truth, it seemed to me, was that so did everyone else I encountered. "Just what would it take to interrupt all this waiting?" I continued to wonder.

As I prepared the pages of this book, I moved through the process of grief after losing my home to a fire. I reflected on my own life and recalled all the great teachers I've encountered. I saw a common thread: Deep down inside, we desire the freedom to be ourselves, to allow *all* of our messy humanity, and to be able to accept the gory as well as the glory in ourselves—and out there in the world.

Now that I've shared some of the experience that shapes a lifetime's expertise in waiting, we will jump into the some of the major areas of life where these disempowering holding patterns (also known as "waiting!") tend to hang around and cause trouble. You will read stories of wisdom from friends, colleagues, and those I admire. We will examine the day-to-day things that keep us stuck, all the while keeping an eye out for that which sneakily runs the show, creating havoc as it does: our pervasive demand for certainty in an uncertain world—for as we wait for certainty, our life passes us by.

Before you turn the page, I will give you the first of a series of "Gentle Knocks" that are spread throughout the book. If you are like me, you might just turn the page and rush on past these opportunities. Instead, I ask you to stop for a moment and contemplate the questions. Have a journal nearby as you read so you can jot down your thoughts, responses, and reactions. Perhaps share what you see with a trusted friend, advisor, coach, or therapist. You will read stories and examples of grappling with the major areas in life where we wait, and by applying these to your own life perhaps you can find some of the freedom you seek.

Gentle Knock:

What are some things that happened during your childhood that you find yourself still carrying around with you? What old behavior (or behaviors) still gets in your way? What is the connection between what happened when you were young and those behaviors that get in your way? What does freedom mean to you? Where have you lost yours? Do you think your fears will ever leave entirely? What if they don't?

Chapter 2:

Great Expectations: Accepting Our True Self

Maturity evolves after you have tried the numerous avenues of escape, only to find that same woundedness still waiting for you.

— GANGAJI

In the last chapter, I told you a bit about who I am and how I got to be this way. And because I have made it my mission to explore the minutiae of what it means to be someone who waits in life, I also have an idea of whom I am talking to—that's you, the reader, my fellow "waiter." In many ways, of course, you and I are not the same. We have had many different formative experiences.

Yet, deep down inside, I know who you are. You are smart, savvy, and successful in many ways, yet dissatisfied on a profound level. You crave freedom, yet you don't ever quite let yourself be. You pick, prod, preach, and still come up short. When will you ever arrive at the place of perfection, you wonder? All the while knowing (because you are smart) that that place doesn't exist. But try to reach it, you will, nonetheless. And you'll lose yourself in the process.

At least that's what happened to me. I tried many avenues of escape. I ran toward some things and away from others. I hoped to flee my mind, my limiting beliefs, my angst, my doubts and fears. I wanted to be fixed! Yet, the harder I tried, the further I ran from me.

The fire that destroyed my house was earth-shaking, life-changing, deeply devastating, and, the experience gave me another opportunity to see where I still lacked acceptance of myself.

On one hand, I did allow myself to grieve and be where I needed to be, yet I also hoped the incident itself would change me. Given the rich metaphors about the transformative aspects of fire, I was disappointed when the same me was still here, day after day, often feeling lost, displaced, yet relentlessly the same—always just on the outside of some marvelous discovery. Conversely, I did change. But I changed due not to the fire, but to my own willingness to allow myself to be where I was. Ironically, I grew by not changing.

Growing by not changing? What on earth does that mean, especially for an expert in the field of self-help, a professional who makes her living helping people grow into positive change?

Here's how that works. A lot of times we wait for people, places, and things. But even sneakier is how we wait for ways of being. For instance, we wait until we "feel better," are more spiritual, more transformed, less scared, more ready...

One day, as I walked through the doors of our local television station to share my tale with the others across Colorado who were dealing with forest fires, a well-meaning friend on the phone offered what he thought were encouraging words, "You can share how you are dealing with this so differently after writing your book about *not* waiting."

I felt myself brace: That's *not* true!

"No!" I said to him. "There is no quick fix for this. I want to share how it's messy and not linear and unpredictable and doesn't have to be anything other than it is, and yet, still, there are moments of beauty." After that I treated him to a bit of a rant about expectations of how we should be, our culture's discomfort with grief, how we celebrate when a grieving process looks all clean and tidy and we return to "normal" relatively quickly.

We have stuck all the messy feelings and reactions of grief into a greeting-card response. I mean, really, why is it we celebrate how "well" someone is doing after a horrible loss? What does that even mean? Like: "She's doing so well since her children died in that horrible crash..." How about we admire emotional messiness, piles of dirty laundry, and heaps of snot?

We want things solved, straightened, wrapped up in a neat package somehow—even when terrible things are happening or have happened. Yet when we ourselves don't feel the same sparkly way during a tough time, we judge our process with vicious and oppressive severity. Why can't we just let ourselves be?

Did I communicate any of that live on air that night? I hope so. I spoke from my heart to the hearts of those who were just beginning to board the frightening ride with the fires across our state that summer. Now I speak it to you, perhaps a little more lucidly since cameras are not rolling and I can go back and edit for more clarity.

My ambition is to provide peace of mind and heart for those who grapple with life. I want ease for those who struggle. But not ease so you can get more quickly to "the other side." Just for the moment, let us not trouble ourselves with getting to the other side. Instead, I want the ease of your own self-acceptance while you are in the midst of your own mess. I am not implying that you need to stay in the muck forever. Just that, when you are there, let yourself be *there*.

After the fire, I made a commitment to *not* know how it would go, to be where I was and *not* come to "the other side" a moment too soon. I promised not to emerge from the cocoon before I was ready. The permission I gave myself was freeing. And, of course, I am not claiming that once I gave myself that permission, I always remembered I had done so. No, I had to keep reminding myself to let myself be. Over and over and over again.

That freedom—to feel and be as I truly was, not as I was supposed to be—was a full deep breath and a level of acceptance I had craved before but never quite knew. If you have ever let yourself dance in your own darkness with some degree of acceptance, you know what I mean. You know the paradox— the relief of letting yourself be *in* it, yet not always *of* it. And, you know equally that this state is not a fixed state. It changes, too—with the wind, with the bumping-up against another angsty human, or even with a bad case of indigestion.

If you don't know that freedom, I invite you to start practicing. Start now, while the waters are calm—or even more challenging, start now if the waters are choppy. You have an opportunity to accept yourself in a way you never have before. The concept of a straight line where you neatly move through stages and emerge victorious—is baloney. The idea that you create an empowering mindset and always, unwaveringly live from that—can we be done with that?

I am about the messy these days. I bare my soul and share my darkness, as well as celebrate the new growth on a burned-out tree, or a hawk flying low, or that when I kiss the velvet forehead of my dog, my heart breaks with love. It is ALL of that.

When we allow ourselves this freedom to be, we can meet each other *there* with knowing looks and a warm embrace. We will see the flotsam and jetsam of darkness and recognize a fellow traveler. We won't brush things over, but we will begin to know what deserves our grappling powers and what doesn't.

Some might label this as a lack of choice. I say everything is a choice, and how and what we choose is intensely personal. I am choosing to be here. I am choosing to ride the wave as it carries me to a soft sandy beach to bathe in the sun. Or as it tosses me against a jagged rock jetty and I am bled dry. I will see where this ride will take me: *this* ride where, if I truly let go, and can stay in this place, and not try control the outcome—where might I end up? I'm not even describing curiosity; it's more like plain vanilla willingness. Nothing fancy, just wanting to see.

Part of being willing to be in the unknown is the challenge of recounting it. And I can't be separate from it right now, so I am describing the experience from down in the trenches of grief and mourning, I am telling you about the blood and the guts and the mud and the bullets whizzing overhead with glimpses of the blue sky. I am not telling you about the battle that was fought twenty years ago and the wisdom I gleaned and now want to pass on from a place on high... No. I am not doing that. God knows we have heard enough of that.

I met a man recently who openly shared his pain with me. A stranger across a counter, he casually mentioned something about life being difficult. I made the split-second decision to bridge the gap between casual conversation and connecting with another soul. If he wanted to be heard, I was ready to listen. He continued on:

> *Two years ago I was in a car accident that almost killed me. I spent three months in the hospital in and out of a coma, slowly healing my broken body. I ran a six-figure business, which quickly went down the tubes without me at the helm. My wife was distraught, having given up her career while we raised our children and being unable to make enough money to pay our bills. After I left the hospital, I still couldn't return to work, and we fell further and further behind. The bank took my house, and then the repo men showed up and carted away all our stuff. We now live with our kids*

—*something I would never have considered before. I work at a hardware store where I make a third of what I used to make. I miss my life before the accident and some nights toss and turn in disbelief at what we have lost, the changes that have happened and my fear about our future.*

At sixty years old, I am not sure if I will ever make it back to where I was before. Some days I wish I could, and other days, I just plain don't want to work that hard. Living with our kids gives us daily time with my grandkids— whom I almost never saw. Working here at this counter, at a store where I once breezed through the aisles on my way back to my busy life, I get to meet new people every day. As I pause to say hello, or to help someone find something they need, I can see the pain in some people's eyes and the joy in others'. Some people stop for a chat and others rush by. For me, everything has slowed down—and sometimes (he was now whispering), I thank God for the accident and a second chance at life.

As he finished, I saw a twinkle of laughter in his eyes, even as tears formed. I felt as if I had seen a sage—someone who had lived and learned and grown—and now had forgiven himself on a deeper level than many of us do. I simply listened during our time together, choosing not to tell him of my recent woes. He knew I understood by my willingness to listen.

Now let's consider how we wait to give ourselves self-acceptance. Think about how you would have reacted to this man's story, and then see how that differs from how you would react if the story had been your own. My guess is you, my enlightened reader, would not shut this man down or feed him an empty "empowering" one-liner. You would not expect him to be somewhere other than where he is. You would have patience with his process and would recognize that sometimes emotional scars take longer to heal than physical scars. Perhaps you would recommit yourself to express unwavering compassion for people's stuck places. Are you willing to offer this kind of generosity to yourself?

As you know, we mainly stick to our well-worn ideas of ourselves, until A) an unexpected challenge calls us to emerge to a bigger, bolder version of ourselves, demands that we take a fresh look at who we can be, or B) we emerge without an emergency by creating our identity and self-acceptance afresh each day—making it our top priority to get curious about who we are and who we can be with a different approach. Either way, we have the opportunity to reflect and connect with our deeper selves.

Gentle Knock:

Here's your chance to offer some acceptance to yourself.

Where are you judging yourself?

Would you judge a stranger the way you judge yourself?

How have unexpected events or changes in your life brought about something completely new—and even wonderful—even though things didn't go as you planned?

The man I met in the store that day was still figuring out his new identity and coming to terms with the demands of his new life, yet he also seemed to have a deep sense of peace that many of us long for. As I reflect on my fortunate meeting with this unusual gentleman, I ask myself what I am asking you: Just how much space and encouragement am I going to give to this richer, rawer self that is emerging? By what standards will I judge my unfolding and therefore unfamiliar new self?

A month after the fire, I wrote the following:

> *Being the seeker that I am, I want to know who I will become. I see parts emerging— some that I will want to keep—and other parts I will want to move through or discard. The truth that coexists is that I want this richer, edgier part of me that is claiming her place in my soul to live on as well. I will take my joys as they come and feel the deep pangs of grief too. But, can I please have a year? Can I have a year to be unwound, to be returning to form, to be in the un-manifested? May I have the space to be inspired or inspiring in one moment and the space to be a lunatic the next? Can society bear that? Can my acquaintances tolerate that? Can my inner circle really be with that? And, most importantly, will I allow myself this space and freedom?*

If we wait for the perfect experience of self-acceptance, we may wait forever. But we can take baby steps. Some days will be easier than others. Some days may be brutally difficult. One of the best ways to approach self-acceptance is to honor those discredited or disowned versions of ourselves—such as "The Little Kid Who Didn't Get to Feel Safe or Play" or "The Hard Worker Who's Always Getting Dissed For Being Too Driven or Busy" or even "The Sensitive Soul Who Bears the Weight of the World." As you already know, we all have a few of these different aspects of self running around in our psyches, and they get especially agitated and freaked out when there's a crisis and they know we aren't going to listen to them and consider their needs. This is one way to explain why we feel so miffed when someone tries to rush us to "empowerment" when all those "selves" really need is some acknowledgement and assurance that they will get to have their say and we will listen.

You can keep waiting for that one day that you do everything perfectly, nothing messily, and always feel good—and you can wait forever. Or today, you can practice a tiny bit of self-acceptance of your desires, needs, and feelings, no matter how messy they might be.

Chapter 3:

Waiting 'til I'm Absolutely Certain

How much of human life is lost in waiting.
— RALPH WALDO EMERSON

We savvy spiritual folk say we know that certainty doesn't exist. We stick magnets on our fridges and bumper stickers on our cars that remind us to embrace the unknown, take the leap, and be willing to fall in our quest for greatness.

However, remember the Chick-a-go incident or the Injury-to-Avoid-Horse-Jumping story? Sure, I was just a kid. But both these moments contain some fundamental fears in which certainty would be a pretty darn nice thing to have: the certainty that I will impress others when I speak and not be ostracized or ridiculed, the certainty that I will not fall off this jumping thousand-pound beast and be judged for doing so.

Deep down, children or adults, we all really do want certainty. We want to know what's going to happen next. We want to know how life will turn out. We desire consistency and routine. We crave the comfort that comes from the familiar. There is nothing wrong with our desire for safety and comfort. In fact, it is crucial to our survival. And we're not talking just about creature comforts. The survival of our species, when we lived in caves and large beasts roamed the land, depended on our being part of a herd. Away from our gang, we were vulnerable to things that had bigger teeth, were fiercer, and wanted to eat us for dinner. This need for safety is hard-wired into us.

Therefore, we resist what is unknown. The unknown is scary. So, we incessantly search for answers, thinking that once we "know," we will arrive at the truth, and then we can relax our guard.

On the day my parents announced their divorce, they ushered my brother and me into my father's study. The words coming out of their mouths were hard for my eight-year-old mind to comprehend. Doing most of the talking, my dad said: "I'm moving to Boston, we will still see each other, I love you very much..." To me, it sounded like the hum of a fan. "What is happening?" I wondered. One minute, I had been happily playing in my room and the next; my dad was saying words that were shredding the fabric of my world into tiny, horribly uncertain strips. Tears stuck in my throat as I choked them down. I wanted to scream "No!" but I stayed silent.

In that one surreal moment all that I thought was certain no longer was. The world no longer made sense. The family I "knew" would always be there no longer existed. It felt like the rug got ripped out from under me. In that moment, I decided I needed to be on alert—high alert, preferably ALL THE TIME—in order to prepare for the next looming disaster.

I'm not sure how concerned I was about knowing things before that day, but after this conversation that need became a central preoccupation. I developed the need to know, the need to find the truth, the need for certainty. I reasoned that, if I had only known about my parents' problems, things might have turned out differently; I could have prevented the divorce. I acquired the erroneous belief that if I could just figure it all out, everything would fall into place. I could stop feeling so unsettled and uncomfortable; I could stop waiting. Life would return to normal. I would feel a sense of certainty; peace would reign in my world. I could put my family back together, and then everything would be OK.

> Small things can set us off—tiny incidents that matter to no one else but loom large in our minds. We latch onto them, magnify them, and they become indelible, forming who we become. Even though these events may have occurred long ago, we get messages, learn lessons, and make decisions that impact our feelings, thinking, and behavior. When we make these formative decisions, we are not always aware that we are altering the course of our lives.

At eight years old, I wasn't conscious of all the decisions I made at that formative moment, yet now, looking back, I can't help but see how irrevocably they shaped my life. What was too painful to feel, I stuffed down inside. Later, I turned to drugs, alcohol, and food to numb my pain. I sought relationships to feel the love I thought I was missing, yet was the first to leave if things looked rocky. Then, after getting into recovery, still searching for answers and hoping to find the truth, I immersed myself in the field of psychology and personal growth.

Yet truth is a moving target. By the time we find what seems to be the truth and identify it as such, what was true in one moment, may not be true in the next. When we define a concept, we also confine it, forcing it to remain fixed within our description. The "truth" then becomes limited to our view, our opinion, and our position.

At some point in my journey of personal development, I began to suspect that the metaphorical "rug" that was yanked out from under me didn't actually exist. I longed to cry foul at this notion, to resist this idea or block it out. I wanted that rug! I needed to know that rug was there. Yet, as I looked around at the upheaval in the world, both past and present, the fact that there didn't seem to be much we could count on besides gravity, death (and taxes, as they say), I began to realize that change is all we can really rely upon, and that life rarely goes the way we plan.

I still yearned for certainty, yet I realized that to accomplish anything outside of my normal realm I had to stretch, grow, and take some risks. Therein lies the rub. What is a seeker to do? If we wait for that illusive rug, or until the coast is clear and all is safe, we will have waited past the time to act. And often, if we wait to know "for sure," we will have waited a moment too long.

The false notion that there was a rug at all was simply my demand for certainty, and the more we demand certainty, the further we are from finding it.

Consider that:

Nothing is solid or predictable.
Nothing will stay the same.
Nothing stays constant.
Everything is in flux.
There are no guarantees.

There are times when it is better to wait until we have more information or a different perspective—that is, to wait until we have more clarity to accurately determine our approach. Like a pilot determining the weather patterns before taking off, we too can take the time to gather information to ensure our flight is a safe one and that we arrive at our destination versus somewhere else entirely. So how can we tell when learning more and being better informed is a good thing, versus the thing that keeps us frozen? Or to put it more bluntly, how can we tell if we are being patient, or if we are being a chicken?

To add salt to the wound, we are faced with having to make decisions daily. Some will alter the course of our lives; others will merely take us to the next point in time. Without the gift of foresight, we must evaluate how something is or looks in a moment and make a decision. We all know how easy it is to look back and second-guess our choice—as from any vantage point there is always the next crest where we can see even more.

And later, on the next peak when everything looks different yet again, we judge the decisions we make. Perhaps viewed from space, it all might make sense, but down here on earth we end up questioning everything.

As we continue the juggling act of dealing with uncertainty, making decisions, and then second-guessing ourselves, we continue to be bombarded with the latest bad news that seems pervasive in our modern world. With all of this, it's no wonder we lose our commitment to staying in the unknown and to taking risks. Part of our quest for certainty involves the question of "why?" Like my own wondering about: *Why do bad things happen? Why do people do the things they do? Why is the world the way it is?*

My psychologist friend Sally shared her story with echoes of my own thoughts:

> *As a therapist since the early '80s, I have seen and heard from many types of people over the years. So often it was easy to see where they were trapped or stuck and to help them find a new tool bag full of techniques to give them a sense of success in life. I felt that I was following my calling, helping people to wake up and live full lives. Many of my clients went on to do great things, beyond their wildest expectations. In my personal life, I balanced out by my love of being outdoors and climbing*

the great mountains all across the country. There was nothing like standing on a summit to put all that ailed me or the world in perspective. Yet, one day after a particularly strenuous climb, I bottomed out. You see, in a moment of sheer exhaustion, I saw something I had been refusing to see before: Even after my years of professional training, all the people I helped along the way, my very full life, I still longed for something I couldn't quite name.

I craved a simple answer to a complicated question: Why? Why must people continue to suffer, why wasn't I deeply happy in my core, why was there so much strife in the world when so many of us were awake? I realized what I wanted—actually, what I demanded— was a sense of certainty. And, in the same moment, I knew it didn't exist. I was waiting for something that would never come, and it was keeping me trapped.

I wish I could say that in the moment of that realization, my life altered forever. However, this wouldn't be true. I resisted the notion of an uncertain world like I resisted catching poison ivy. I realized that not only did this show up in my personal life, but that I also wanted to give my clients some sort of certainty in their lives.

Slowly allowing myself to grasp how uncertain everything is, and how the only thing I can do about this is accept it, became my biggest gift. Now I help others to come to their own sense of freedom about this underlying truth of our human existence. To live fully is often to be in the unknown.

Most likely we will never get the answer to the "why?" And it looks as if we will never get the demand for certainty that so many of us seek.

Gentle Knock:

What would be possible if you were willing to let go of your need to know?

What, if anything, are you certain about?

In what areas of life does lack of certainty most bother you?

How important is "being right"? People often say that it's more important to be happy than to be right. How does that idea feel to you?

When we become willing to stop waiting for certainty, we open ourselves to the unknown, which may be terrifying, yet it can lead to new places, people, and ideas. As we learn to let go, there may be claw marks where we were holding on, but on the other side we can find freedom. And this isn't a one-time shot. Most of us have to release our need to know over and over again. We let it go, we pick it back up. We release, and then we hold on more tightly. We breathe a sigh of relief, and then we clench our jaws. We remember and then we forget.

That is the human condition—to remember and forget and remember all over again. That is the journey of this book. When we spend more time remembering and less time forgetting, maybe then we will have released our need for certainty. If only a little bit.

Chapter 4:

Holy Non-Attachment

Don't put Mout' on it.

— BAHAMIAN WISDOM

I f you travel between the small islands of the Bahamas, you might hear a subtle warning. This underlying cultural message is pretty much the opposite of the done-to-death teachings on the law of attraction so popular in our American climate of positive thinking. Coming from those who spend so much time on and near the capricious sea, "Don't put Mout' on it" suggests we don't tout the positive, as we just might jinx ourselves. In other words, don't count your chickens until they are hatched. Many boaters subscribe to this belief system, not wanting to curse themselves in any way when so far from shore.

Do I believe this? I'm not sure. But I do know, as I sail in uncharted waters, I will not be overly cocky. And it's an "interesting" coincidence that, in the year I declared to be "the year of letting go of attachments," my house burned to the ground. I don't think I will tempt fate like that again. Ever. Arguably, one of the biggest attachments I had was to my beloved home.

It seems that, for those of us on a spiritual path, the concept of non-attachment is a heralded place. The root questions seem to be: Why do some "have" while others do not? Is it bad to have and good to have not? Should the "havees" take care of the have-nots? Our Western concepts of non-attachment are influenced by centuries of asceticism and comfort-denial in our own religious heritage, which are based on the premise that, the more discomfort you experience in this life (poverty, hair-shirts, starvation, etc.), the better you're going to have it in the next, or the closer you will be to God. The Dalai Lama himself tells us that attachment is the root of all suffering.

We claim we don't want to suffer, and certainly we want to be good and fair people, so therefore it seems we should strive for non-attachment. Thankfully, after coming from extreme privilege and then trying the path of extreme self-denial, the

Buddha points to a middle way. Still, where we should fall on this attachment continuum is not an easy question to answer— even after the majority of my physical attachments vanished.

After the fire, quite a few well-meaning people mused aloud about how freeing it must be to lose all your stuff. Now, I certainly understand what they meant. (And, on a separate note, this is one of the things you should avoid saying to a fire victim. Until we are ready to feel the "freedom" ourselves, it is best to keep those musings silent.)

I have always liked my things. Losing all of them did not make me like them any less. And, I can't say that I felt any freer—at least, not right away.

Losing everything to a fire does not automatically instill a philosophy of non-attachment. No, it brings sadness, pain, loss, and confusion. It also brings extreme fatigue coupled with reams of paperwork. It brings negotiations with faraway folks behind desks who depreciate prized possessions by 75 percent or greater. However, it is also true if I hadn't been so attached to my things, my clothes, my treasured possessions, and particularly my house, I wouldn't have suffered quite so much.

Metaphorically, it may be freeing to have no stuff. Realistically, it is a pain in the butt. It is heartbreaking to recall the disintegrated items. It is devastating to comprehend the great loss. And, to have to list all the items you ever owned for insurance purposes is downright awful.

This experience is a death, a trauma, an extreme shock to the system. My muscle memory is still intact and the sensations created in my beloved home come rushing back in total recall. How it felt to sit on my leopard chaise curled up in a blanket next to the cool pane of my French door while sipping my first cup of coffee; the walk down the stairs holding the smooth railing as I went for my four a.m. pee; the texture of the beloved desk in my office where I doodled as I talked to clients; that deep cellular sense of relaxation and safety as I snuggled into MY bed—all these memories still exist in my body. One day something I loved was there, and the next it was gone. Our systems take a little while to catch up to this fact.

We were warned we would remember things that had fallen into the shadows of memory and that these things would emerge at the strangest of times. Seemingly shrouded in fog forever, abruptly they would materialize and shock us awake. "Holy Non-Attachment" was one of the best responses I received when telling someone my house burned down. Holy non-attachment is right!

Let me show you how the experience of "No Stuff" showed up in my day-to-day life. In essence, it was a prolonged and repeated feeling of missing. In those early days, I cast about for what was familiar, only to find *nothing* was. I missed my snow boots—much needed in the early April snowstorm that broke the drought of March. I wondered: *Where is my sunscreen, my small strainer to drain the coffee grounds, the spoon that measured just the right amount of agave for my coffee? Where is my favorite lip balm, my paddle brush that didn't rip my hair, my supply of gold hair elastics? Where are my delicate laundry bags to wash my bras, my favorite pair of socks, and my other slipper?*

I had the chance to grab a few things before fleeing, one of which was my single slipper, but for a while I was sure I had grabbed both. Upon the realization that I now had just one, the torrent of more wondering came pouring through my brain: *Where is the purple hat my dad gave me, my wooly scarf I wore even in the summer? Where is the purple down throw I snuggled with in my living room? Where is my stockpile of favorite lotion they stopped making? Where is the soapstone box that David gave me, the puppy picture of my beloved dog Jaxson? Where is my Blendtec blender with which I kept up with my necessary vegetable consumption, my new green protein powder from Whole Foods, my huge supply of almond butter, my mint tea? Where are my sweatpants, my hiking boots, and my iPod?*

And it's not just the stuff. I missed the routines of having a home. Even now, it seems like a bad dream. Freedom from suffering, that perfect non-attachment zone of the Dalai Lama, was not at all what this experience offered early in the game.

The pathos of the loss—and its apparent ridiculousness at times—grabbed me at the strangest and most inappropriate times. In the vegetable aisle during my first trip to Safeway after the fire, I thought of my blue plastic Q-tip holder, and I completely lost it—hysterically sobbing, bent over at the waist, unable to walk another step. My husband, David, ran to pat my head. I recovered momentarily; then lost it again one aisle over.

Now, this Q-tip holder had never been that special to me, but its loss symbolized so much. After telling this story to my friends, my goddess friend Dusty bought me Q-tip holder filled with Q-tips. I still treasure it. She said she wandered the store for an hour trying to think of what to get me, all the while carrying this simple plastic holder. She thought, towels, pillows, something, what, what, what should she get me... She left with only the Q-tip holder. I love my new Q-tip holder. For so long, we didn't want towels, or pillows, or anything bigger. We had no place to put it. The idea of accumulation was troubling. During our time of living in basements, hotels, and the trailer, we were never sure where we were going to live next, where we would end up, or if we would re-build. We didn't know anything. I liked my Q-tip holder because I knew I could carry it with me. I could still get out fast with it if I needed to.

I have shared some of my relationship to and connection

with stuff. Now I will give you the opportunity to look at your own attachments.

Gentle Knock:

Take a quick inventory of your "stuff." How much is in storage? How much new stuff do you acquire every year? What percentage of your stuff would you say you haven't looked at or touched in the last year? Last three years? Last five years?

Do you stockpile stuff for a rainy day? Or stockpile projects you know you'll never get to?

How attached do you feel to your stuff? Do you think it's wrong to have such attachments?

One morning, after the fire, I remembered something that fell into the "priceless" category of my stuff, something that could never be replaced. When I was eight years old, my beloved babysitter, Mrs. Vogler, fashioned a sturdy stool made from steel cans, covered in padded velvet with a golden tassel and an embroidered "K" for Kristen. I carried this stool with me through my various moves across the country, between households and into my own home. I still used it regularly. It was good for reaching tall cabinets or taking a brief respite in the midst of a busy day.

When I remembered the stool, the dam almost broke. Too early, not enough coffee, and not wanting to feel the pain, I felt the sob emerge and swallowed it whole. Irreplaceable, a memory lost in a fiery flame, Mrs. Vogler's stool might not make the dreaded insurance "inventory list." It made the short list of things I really missed—treasures of a lifetime.

Freedom is an interesting concept. We all have different ways in which we feel free. I am not saying I don't understand the impulse to wax poetic about freedom after loss, but when you really look at it, isn't it silly? We know (intellectually) that stuff doesn't make us happy. We have given up the '80s notion that "he who dies with the most toys wins."

If you ask a homeless woman whose possessions fit in a shopping cart if she is freer, what answer might she give? How about the serial dater who swears off getting serious? Are they free? Is everyone who has had a taste of spiritual enlightenment free? Are the young and innocent freer? Are the aged and wizened freer?

Some people work in jobs they hate and feel they don't have any freedom, but to quit or change jobs might result in a more threatening loss of money, which means less freedom still. Some people seem to have every access to freedom gifted by abundant circumstances and yet seem the most trapped of all. And we have heard tales of prisoners who have transformed their lives and experienced freedom of spirit behind bars.

What does this freedom thing really mean? Freedom to come and go? Freedom to be who we want to be? Freedom to pick up and leave at any moment? Freedom to do as we wish? Freedom to speak and write without fear of censorship or worse? Freedom to make mistakes? Freedom to marry the one we love? Freedom to do what we want with our bodies? Freedom to bear arms or have our arms be bare?

And how does not having Mrs. Vogler's stool make me freer?

I am not saying I have the answer to this. I am exploring. I am remaining curious as I ride the wave and wonder who I will become. When I crash in the surf and lose sight of the shore, I am more interested in breathing than in the transformation that will come. And, in those moments of catching the perfect ride, I see glimpses of who I want to be. But is that out there on the horizon? Is freedom out there, waiting for me to arrive? Is it as easy as shifting right now? Grief is a process. Life is a process. Looking back in time since the fire, I can see signs of the different stages I moved through. Those early days are a blur. When the numbness wore off and some of the heavy sadness lifted, moments of disbelief continued to rush to the surface. I often wondered, "What are we doing again? How did we get here? Where is my house? Why am I living in a basement?" The desire to go home, to *that* home, was strong.

As the days passed, I learned to find freedom in the little things. One clear, crisp day, under the blaring Colorado sun, we met with a forestry expert to determine the fate of the scorched trees on our barren land. Glancing up at two we hoped to save but that were, sadly, on the "fell" list, we paused. "What is that?" we wondered aloud. "Is that what we think it is?" It was. A small patch of green pine needles way up high, almost beyond seeing. Was it a trompe l'oeil or the small sign of hope? Since we both saw it, and then the kind man who would fell the rest saw it, we believed it to be true. It was new growth. A few clumps of green amidst a sea of black and grey. These two trees were our favorites besides our long-lost pine that towered over our deck and provided much-needed shade on our south-facing lot. Shade is a missing commodity on our land, and during the hot summer days of Colorado it would be intolerable to live there without it.

Will those two trees come back fully? We don't know. Officially, they were given a stay of execution.

The nice young man who was to fell our trees knew what he was doing. He was fifteen when his family lost their home in a forest fire. First he and his brother helped their parents cut down their own beloved trees. After proving his skill, the neighbors caught wind, and he was hired out to cut down their trees during their recovery process. Later, when most youngsters are still unsure of what to do with their lives, he was clear. He would start a business preserving and maintaining forests with a specialization in helping others after the horror of a forest fire. Our local resource center passed his name along after he offered his services at a discount to all of us who suffered. At twenty-seven, he carried wisdom far beyond his years. He patiently followed me around as I became more and more willing to let more and more trees go. As we examined the trees, he explained to me, "We call them 'widow makers' after a fire. The tree still stands but its insides are structurally compromised due to the burn. You never know when one might drop, either while you sleep or as you innocently pass by. It's not uncommon to hear of people being injured or killed in this way." With that sobering information, we knew we had to say goodbye to our trees.

I was relieved to put our forest health in this young man's hands—he understood as one who lost his own home and as the expert he had become.

When he finished telling me his story, I asked this man what was the biggest life lesson he received after his fire.

His reply: "It's all just stuff."

A good metaphor for all of life. *It's all just stuff.* Sometimes I will interact with it like that—and other times I won't. And I will attempt to grasp the ungraspable, which is just like herding cats.

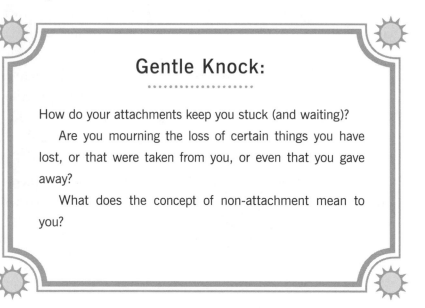

Gentle Knock:
· · · · · · · · · · · · · · · · · ·

How do your attachments keep you stuck (and waiting)?

Are you mourning the loss of certain things you have lost, or that were taken from you, or even that you gave away?

What does the concept of non-attachment mean to you?

One thing is certain—the fire brought my relationship to material possessions into vivid and uncanny focus. I now view objects that could be mine with a whole new apprehension and respect. Will I ever want more than will fit in the back of my car with my two big dogs and my cat? For a while, the answer was a resounding "no!" and even now, settled into our new home with new things, I look around and wonder, "Where did this stuff come from? Whose is it? Whose home am I in? Will I lose it all again?"

Maybe freedom is in the moments when we remember, or stop, or breathe deeply. It's not an arrival or a destination. If we are fighting for freedom or the right to be free, then there could be a moment of demarcation where freedom becomes possible, but then it becomes up to each individual to exercise that freedom. We can be given freedom and not take it. We can be born into freedom and not experience it. Ask any teenager if they feel free, and most likely the response will be a grunted "No." They feel the bondage of living under their parents' roof.

We wizened ones will scoff at this and say, "They don't even begin to know what lack of freedom means." But do we adults know so much better? Maybe none of us do. Freedom is the access to rights, but it is frequently experienced in the lacking of those rights—a new passion for freedom is born.

Gentle Knock:

Where does freedom live for you? Where do you take it for granted and what recent wake-up calls have encouraged you to reconsider? Is freedom a fleeting moment or a place of residence? Is it a deep exhale? Is it the glint of the sun on the surf in Borneo, or the glimmer of wicked humor in your friend's eye? Is it the right to vote, to learn, to express, to marry, to carry?

At least I am free of the worry of who will sort through all my stuff when I die. I will have stuff again, just not so much. I won't need to fret about someone worrying about what to do with my old journals, scrapbooks, or mementos. They are all gone, for good. I am free of *that* concern. But rest assured, plenty of other concerns have taken its place. Does that mean I am not free? Is someone reading my words somewhere out there, shaking his or her head, thinking, "She hasn't gotten it. She doesn't understand"? Maybe. Is he or she freer than I? I don't know.

If I could go back in time, I *would* grab more stuff. I wouldn't grab all of it, but there would be certain things like puppy pictures of our beloved Jaxson, my snow boots, David's coin collection—and, of course, Mrs. Vogler's stool.

Keepsakes and mementoes connect us to significant times. They bring us back and remind us of who we once were and on many occasions how far we have come. I still had a selection of love letters from my significant relationships before I met David. This didn't threaten my husband, and I am sure he had some as well. Of course, I kept the handwritten collection of poems from David—including the first he wrote me one week after we met. Fortunately, some of these are digital, but many aren't. Ah, all the things we hold on to, cling to, deem necessary...

I thought these mementos were vital. They grounded me in a past, they demonstrated I was loved; they showed a reflection of me in others' eyes over the years.

What do they prove? Nothing, really. Who am I without them? Everything I ever was—and more.

If my new house was on fire, there would definitely be some things I would want to carry out. But if I didn't have any of them, I would be OK. I am certainly not suggesting you have a fire to cure your attachments to stuff or things. I would not recommend that! But how many favorite things can we actually have? If it's not a favorite thing, then really, why do we have it? And, it's not that I don't love my stuff anymore. I do. I still want nice things. The difference is that I now know from experience that most everything is replaceable. Lives are not.

Gentle Knock:

Speaking of lighting a fire… If your house was burning down and you had thirty minutes to get out, what would you take in an evacuation? What would you leave? Make a list.

Look back at this list. What can you do without? What really matters to you? Why does it matter?

For most human beings, our stuff (or lack of stuff) plays a significant part in our identity, our ideas about who we are, and our expressions of what's most important to us. How does the stuff of your life help shape and define and express you? How or who would you be if it was altered or removed in some way?

The truth is, even if I didn't have what matters most to me—my dogs and David—ultimately, someday in the far distant future, I would be OK. I say that now, but do I really believe it? I am certainly not asking for *that* lesson! Yet here lies the depth of the human spirit. We are resilient creatures. Our minds will tell us otherwise, but in our bones we know our power. We have to nurture this part of ourselves.

This is the true freedom—the freedom to be at home with ourselves and in ourselves. There is no quick answer to this. There are no "five easy steps" to freedom. And, as we walk through life—and as long as we don't give up—we get stronger with every step.

As it turned out, this past summer was replete with opportunities for me to examine my relationship to what feels most important. In addition to the sudden disappearance of my house, I also had the chance to say goodbye and loosen my attachment to another home. This one, however, we chose to sell. My parents bought the place together in 1971, and the plan was we would keep it *forever*. Since forever doesn't exist, and life priorities change, my family decided to sell it.

We hear that non-attachment is a choice. Well, yes it is. Probably, a choice I get to make over and over again. But I have to say that idea of non-attachment still seemed too devoid of feeling, rigid and stark. When I shared my resistance to selling this home with a beloved friend, she proposed another word instead—"fluidity"—and something settled inside me. Fluidity is something I can wrap my mind around. Non-attachment clearly does not inspire me. I was trying to make it work, I thought I was "supposed to," but I am done with that. Fluidity, on the other hand, speaks to my soul. Of course, there is overlap and connection. Fluidity means movement and ease and light dancing on water. It means I can let go of my belief that I need to be rooted and grounded and planted somewhere. It means that no decision is wrong, as I can merely flow from one to the next. It means tides washing in and bathing everything clean. It means something different at every moment, as I know by watching the waves crash at the beach. No pattern is the same, no wave identical, and no gleam of sunlight on water reproduced.

That makes me sigh deeply. Fluidity, I can work with.

In times of angst, we could ask ourselves, what would fluidity do? I let the question bathe my tired brain. I allow it to soothe my jagged edges. I feel its truth down deep. Fluidity would breathe and expand and sparkle. Fluidity would allow the ups and downs of life. Fluidity would give us a freedom to be where we are.

With fluidity, I could let go on a level I never have before. Our Colorado house was taken from us. Our family home, we are choosing to let go of. They are very different experiences. With this house, I was able to walk from room to room and say my goodbyes. I chose to sweep it out one last time, even though the cleaners were coming later. I did this to honor the house and welcome the new owner. I did this to complete the past, as it was my assigned task that I despised for so long.

After sweeping the whole place, I moved from room to room and ran my hand along the walls, thanking the house for holding us so dearly, remembering snippets of life as I did. Each time a sob started, something came to ease its jaggedness. Opening the closet one last time, I discovered a pile of towels I meant to pack. Cursing David momentarily for putting the towels away after the laundry, I then appreciated the distraction from my pain. Something else caught my attention; a trapped bird was frantically fluttering against a window, trying to get out. Quickly, grabbing a forgotten towel, I was able to catch the bird gently, momentarily meet its frightened gaze, and release it outside.

I wrote this as I moved through those places and spaces, as I said goodbye to my family home.

The last morning: It's turning pink outside, the light reflecting on the clapboard side of this lovely house. Seriously, I think my heart will crack. The pain stabs my chest and throat and I wonder if I can take it. Damn. So, I am someone who attaches to houses, that much is clear.

Places stay solid where people can't. And,

yes, I know I have the ultimate in best people in my life. It's not that I don't know that. I am just wrestling with the illusion of certainty. The illusion that something that feels and appears solid really is. That it might last forever, where people don't, won't, or can't. This place simply holds me right now. Nothing changes, it doesn't have moods, it won't snap at me one moment and be kind the next.

Do I sound like someone who has gotten the lesson in non-attachment? Yeah, I don't think so either... But I am facing it, as I knowingly say goodbye to this beloved place when I never had the chance to say goodbye to my last one.

All of this comes on the eve of where we might land next. It's a dreamy, artsy place where, in my mind, I have already placed many of my precious items from here on shelves. Right now, still, strongly, I want to stay in this room, in this house that I know and love so well. I want to live in this little town where everyone knows each other and I have a history that is older than I am. My great-grandparents are buried in the cemetery here. My grandparents lie next to them.

I wonder, as the pink turns to gold and now it begins to warm the grass, "Are we making the biggest mistake of our life?" A neighbor cat prowls across the lawn and returns victorious with a mouse in his craw. I will await the packers, who hopefully are highly skilled in dealing with people like me whose heart breaks at the sound of the tape gun.

"I am a funny girl," I say. I scream to God and get no answer, yet the answers surround me. As I write my words and share my pain, I have a lightness that wasn't there before. My sadness is here, but it's not threatening to swallow me whole. I am looking at the pink turning to yellow outside and seeing the beauty and knowing I can carry it with me. It is time for another goodbye, yet I won't leave claw marks as I go. Instead, I will shut the door and feel the weight of my ancestors' hands on my mine.

And instead of closing, the door is opening to what is next, what will come, and what will be.

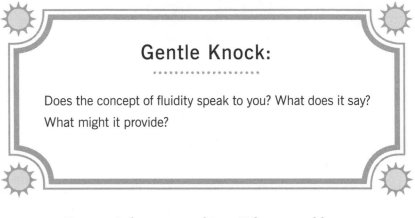

Gentle Knock:

Does the concept of fluidity speak to you? What does it say? What might it provide?

You can't have everything. Where would you put it?

— STEVEN WRIGHT, COMEDIAN

A few months after the fire, while we were still living in our trailer, I had a realization that this time of my life was precious. It was dirty, raw, ash-covered, and tremendously challenging—and it was also precious. I knew that a year from then, we would rejoin the majority by living in a house, and life would be different. We would no longer have to say "Excuse me" to pass by each other. We would have a sink larger than a shoebox. We would shower standing up instead of having to pour water over our heads while seated. And, we would even have a washing machine so we didn't have to do the smell test and ponder: Can I get away with one more day?

Right now, life no longer looks the same. It has similar elements, yet the foundation has changed. Our time spent in basements, hotels, and the trailer was a time of grasping, hoping, and expanding. It gave me a perspective on my life and life in general. It cemented some things I believed in and made me question more. I realized on a deep level that we could wait forever until we accumulate just the "right" stuff and then still feel the void. What ultimately fills that ache inside? Is it OK to still want stuff? Can we let ourselves have it all—stuff and a commitment to non-attachment? I am not going to bash stuff. I like my new stuff. I miss my old stuff. I want more stuff. And, I want to connect on a deeper level to who I really am. To who we really are.

We are part of a bigger whole. We are not alone. We have our connections with our people. And we meet more along the way. We understand each other as we walk through this fire called life and the resulting ups and downs. We stumble and fall along the way. Then we look up for an instant, and perhaps catch a glimpse of green in a towering pine that once was grand, and know one day it may be again.

Chapter 5:

Waiting for Love to Come Along

*After a while you learn
the subtle difference between
holding a hand and chaining a soul*
— "AFTER A WHILE"
BY VERONICA A. SHOFFSTALL

I love my husband. He is up before the sun, making coffee and writing his blog—and these are not the only reasons I love him. I love him because he is a very good man. He is someone I am proud to go through this life with. Besides the very occasional melee (which you'll read about in a minute), we really didn't fight much after the fire—and believe me, the frenetic and anxious energy of that time provided much fertile ground for fighting. By some alchemical miracle we have pulled together and are walking through our fire side by side.

I look into his tired eyes and see my own. I read his thoughtful words and allow them to alter me. I watch him cry as he thinks about how lucky I was to get out alive and the tragedy of the loss of our neighbors. When I am too tired to think and the world seems very, very dark, he pats my head. We crack up at each other's jokes no matter how bad they are. And we experience pure joy as we watch our dogs' ongoing antics—the ultimate proof of goodness in life.

We have more space for each other than usual. In the regular course of events, we get along well, but often have little spats that sound like, "You stepped on my toe!" "No, you stepped on mine!" "Well, you did it first…" Perhaps you have your own version, your own special take on the ludicrous eternal argument of "He Said, She Said…" But strangely enough, since the fire, this type of exchange has been noticeably absent from our repertoire.

Stress can rip people apart—and clearly it can bond people more deeply. When a couple stands at the altar and says, "For richer or poorer, 'til death do us part," how many imagine what will test the promise as life continues on its unpredictable path?

David and I have walked through so many "things" in our years together: cross-country moves, pregnancy losses, deaths of close friends, career changes, the ups and downs of addiction recovery, serious medical conditions, IRS audits—and now fire. There were a few times when we wondered if we could stay together, when all seemed to be crumbling apart.

We didn't use those traditional words when we crafted our own vows—unfortunately, our hand-written vows met their fiery death in our wedding scrapbook so I can't tell you precisely what they were—yet the basic sentiment remained the same.

At that oh-so-important moment when couples declare their commitment, the stats of divorce prove many people *don't* really mean "no matter what." We give ourselves a "back door," as my beloved Lon and Sandy Golnick taught us in their relationship workshop. We say we will stay, we are committed, but what we really mean is, "Well, I will stay, at least until you do that one thing that I really can't tolerate..."—which may be anything from wearing muddy shoes in the house one too many times to repeated infidelity.

All couples go through life's ups and downs, and during particularly challenging times, it became apparent that David and I really meant it when we chose each other. Perhaps even more important, we have continued to choose *us* through thick and thin. We also know when to say uncle and call in the troops. (David and I frequently reach out for support, like relationship coaching with Lon and Sandy.) What we learned is how to close all our "back doors," to truly be in our partnership together. We have had plenty of much-needed support along the way, which has equipped us to take this wild and woolly ride together.

But it wasn't always like this.

Until I got into recovery, I was convinced there wasn't enough love to go around, and I found "proof" everywhere. No matter how many men I dated, no matter how many love letters I received, I couldn't get enough love—or the right kind of love—to *make* me feel complete.

As a teenager, I boldly pasted the poem "After a While" by Veronica A. Shoffstall on the wall of my room. Over and over I read the line that gently suggests to *"Plant your own garden and decorate your own soul instead of waiting for someone to bring you flowers."* I would be independent! I would not give my heart away too easily! I wouldn't wait for a man (or boy)! But wait I did. I indulged in the fantasy of wanting someone to complete me. I waited for my Prince Charming, *the one* who could ride in, sweep me off my feet, carry me off to a beautiful, love-filled, Technicolor life—and save me from myself.

In addition to looking for the wrong thing, I searched in the wrong places. I thought if I slept with a man, he would fall in love with me. While that occasionally led to a relationship, it usually left me feeling empty and ashamed.

On the other extreme, I dated a lot of jealous men. "If only my boyfriend (whichever one it happened to be at the time) didn't need so much reassurance," I reasoned, "the relationship might work." Secretly, I felt their jealousy validated me. It showed I was important and loved—and *worthy* of the jealousy. Although I complained about their jealousy and neediness, all along I hid my own.

If there was any sign the relationship was ending, I was out the door. I knew what it was like to *feel* abandoned. I carried out my childhood vow when my father left: never to be left again. Yet I wondered why most of my relationships didn't work out.

We say we want love, but instead of cultivating it internally, we wait for Prince (or Princess) Charming to arrive and to do it for us. We think their arrival marks the end of emptiness. Never again will we feel alone. And we expect them to be perfect and provide all our needs. We pretend we don't do this, but deep down we do. A lot.

Joanna, a drop-dead gorgeous mother of three, shares her story:

> *After years of dating, I met my husband, James. He was my perfect match. ambitious, responsible, and wanting a family. We married quickly. Three kids, a new business,*

and a move across country later, we started to have difficulties. One day, I ran into my high school sweetheart. Newly divorced, he was as handsome as ever. We were on and off throughout school, and I always had felt he was "the one." Yet we never were in the same place long enough to really have a relationship, so it became something that loomed in the background, in my mind from time to time where I fantasized about him. What began as a semi-innocent coffee date turned into an affair that almost ripped my marriage apart. I finally told my husband, unsure if I would stay or go, and after some horrible weeks of fighting, we went into counseling. I am not saying it was easy, but I realized that my family was more important to me than attempting to start a "new life" with my childhood love. My husband struggled for quite a while with forgiveness, and things were rocky for a while. Then, we moved on—and moved again to our dream town in the mountains.

Now, eight years later, we have it all. Our business is thriving, our kids are amazing, we have built our dream house—and I look around and feel dissatisfied again. Occasionally my husband gets into a dark place about our past and his feelings of betrayal. At these times, I want to run away. Right now, our business is about to be bought by another company, which will set us up financially for life. My husband is stressed to the max, and I am feeling neglected. I am angry and wonder if he will ever be able to give me what I want on an emotional level. He showers me with expensive gifts—but this isn't what I want. Don't get me wrong, I love what he has given me, but I crave a deeper connection emotionally.

After a huge fight where my husband brought up divorce, I was shocked into a new realization! I saw that no one could ever satisfy my deep need—not my first husband, not my second, and not my childhood sweetheart. The only one who could do this for me was me. I was waiting for James to "complete me" and was furious at him for not being able to do so. I decided to get into therapy to deal with my relationship with myself. There still may be things I want to be different in our marriage—and I realized that, until I could be

at peace with myself, I would never be happy.
Now, when I feel those old feelings of dissat-
isfaction surface, I gently remind myself to
return to center.

After getting into recovery, I finally learned to cultivate a
relationship with myself and became responsible for my
own happiness. I learned to look for what I wanted in a man
versus looking to see if he liked me. I wish I could say that
once I learned this lesson, I never needed to learn it again, but
for most of us wisdom doesn't necessarily interrupt ancient
patterns and old habits for once and for all. Now I know that
David isn't responsible for my happiness, but sometimes I want
him to be. Now I realize what love is and isn't, but sometimes
I can forget. Now I know I am complete whether in or out of a
relationship, but I still sometimes swoon at the line from *Jerry*
McGuire where Tom Cruise declares to Renée Zellweger,
"You complete me."

I met my husband a year before we started dating. I spotted
him across the room. Inexplicably, I found myself wanting to
be near him. Sure, he was nice to look at, but it was more than
that. I've seen (and dated) plenty of attractive men. So what
was it about him? It was a "peaceful, easy feeling." It was
something I can't quite describe. I wanted to *know* this man.
We bumped into each other several times over the next year,

and one day he asked for my phone number. I had no fear or doubt; I just knew he would call. On our second date, he handed me a poem:

I saw an Angel today.
I know because she left a golden thread in my car.
I saw it fall as she stepped out,
As if purposefully placed.
So I would not forget she had come.
Or maybe so I would not think it a dream.
But there is no dream to compare to this.
For me she has landed,
I know I saw the gods smile.

We came together as two equals. We chose each other. We took time to create and design our relationship, to understand and align our dreams and goals. We developed a deep friendship. We shared a spiritual path and a life of sobriety.

David may not "complete me," but we do stand side by side for this new phase of our life. We have no idea what the future will hold and sometimes feel incapable of imagining the gifts that may come. Yet we know we will be stronger as individuals and stronger in our love. We celebrate each other, read each other's words, comfort each other's pain, hold each other's hand, and fall asleep side by side. We are aligned on so many things, most importantly the willingness to allow life events to shape us into better people. Tragedy *should* wake us up and remind us to be better people, to live for what really matters versus all the minutiae of a "busy" life. David and I promise to allow this tragedy to remind us of how precious life is and how quickly it can alter.

We have already discussed the human obsession with guarantees—and there is perhaps no arena where we crave certainty so desperately as in the realm of love. From all the love stories and songs that surround us, we know how love is supposed to go. Yet, how it is *supposed* to go is usually not how it *actually* goes.

To further complicate matters, deep down, we are afraid of being alone. Despite our desire for love, we don't often know how to let love in. Fear of abandonment causes many people to go through life protecting their hearts and never knowing true intimacy. Allowing someone to know us, letting them draw close, exposes us to the possibility of being hurt, so we don't share who we really are—we protect our soft underbellies and put on our hard, glittery, most impressive outer shells.

We also see relationships as the end result. We wait until we're in them to be happy. We tell ourselves, "When I get *there*, everything will be OK. When I have my first boyfriend, first kiss, first love, get married, have a child (or two)… Then I will have everything I want." We get the relationship, the newness wears off, the luster fades, and we often blame our partner for failing to meet our expectations. "Was *this* what I was waiting for? Is this all there is? Don't you know I deserve something better?"

We make up rules (often forgetting we made them up, or oblivious to their initial unconscious creation) and then fail to inform our partners—we expect them to know how to behave because, after all, they *said* they loved us! We believe they should follow our rules, and we become resentful when they don't. Our expectations are usually proportionate to the depth of our relationships—often the closer we are to someone, the higher our expectations. (Have you ever had the thought: "He knows me so well—he should get it by now without my having to say what I need all over again…"?)

Speaking of expectations that David would always meet my every need…

And now the already promised "humdinger" of a fight. I liken going through trauma to a chronic and *very* bad case of PMS. Thin-skinned, thrown by the slightest curve ball, excessively sensitive, unpredictably dark—and very, very tired— that is how I would describe myself at that time. David says he now understands what PMS feels like—and, ladies, I believe he does.

Like any couple, we have our ups and downs. During the trying months after the fire, we tried to be as gentle as possible with each other. Then sometimes we'd clash like we did on our way back from a lovely reprieve of camping in southern Colorado. I'm not sure exactly how it started. We were tired, both anticipating traveling for business the next day, and experiencing a normal case of Sunday blues after a long road trip. He said something, I said something, and we began to do the familiar routine. He was sure he was right, and I was equally convinced the truth was on my side.

Of course, it is human nature to want to be right. Most arguments start with small issues and escalate. Problems grow more firmly entrenched the longer we hold our positions. We gather evidence, adding fuel to the fire, and over time, we lose sight of the original issue. What we are left with is, at best, distance in a relationship, and at worst, no relationship at all.

When I believe I am right, I spend an exorbitant amount of time rehashing the situation in my mind. I obsessively review the other person's responses and actions to find the evidence I need. In this internal dialogue, nothing changes. I try to build my case, yet I get nowhere. If I continue down this path, when the time comes to discuss the matter with the other person, I've already become the judge, jury, and executioner.

We call that "righteousness" and I am blessed with my fair share of that devilish trait. Here's what it looks like: We are so sure that our version of the truth is the truth that we block out all other possibilities and kill off any affinity we might have had for the other person. I have my "truth" and you have yours, and rarely do they meet. Just ask any juror who's asked to find that ultimate truth. We all see things in life differently and it's actually quite miraculous when we have any agreement at all on what we see.

Yet we rarely live from this awareness. Instead, we assume that others see things the way we do, and if they aren't agreeing with us we label them as wrong. Add in anger and judgment, and the whole system bogs down. We know that it feels horrible to be at the other end of someone's judgment, especially when we can't understand its source or reconcile his or her version of reality. Yet we continue to do this to others. Factor this out a few levels and we can comprehend how war starts and continues. Absolute commitment to a point of view coupled with a refusal to see that just maybe, possibly, we are seeing only from our eyes—and that it isn't the entire "truth"—is the downfall of humanity.

Unfortunately, in this particular moment, my righteousness and his coincided perfectly. Neither of us had the perspective to pull out of our nosedive and instead steamed for the rest of the ride home. My own steam quickly started to spiral. A house doesn't make a marriage, but it certainly can create a sanctuary where marriage resides. Our mountain home was one such sanctuary. Without it, we were a bit unplugged, to say the least. In this particular moment, I felt a cavernous hole where once, it seemed, was our life. Without the house as glue, would we stick? Could we stick? In these heated moments it is crystal-clear why many couples blow apart in times of crisis. One thing leads so abruptly to the next and before you know it you are saying horribly damaging things like "it's over," and you actually believe it's true. These particular words didn't leave our lips but they swirled in our heads—or they certainly swirled in mine.

All of this bickering while feeling lost kicked up my abandonment issues. At times of great distress with another human being, the first place I land is, "You will leave me." I know the roots: Dad "leaving" when I was eight. And yes, there were all sorts of extenuating circumstances in his decision, but try telling that to an eight-year-old. Try telling that to a tired, worried, triggered forty-six-year-old.

I have learned (through trial and error) that it's best not to lead with, "So, you gonna leave me?" The heat-of-the-moment answer won't bring any comfort to my angsty soul. I do my best to practice the long-respected spiritual principle of "shut up" without saying these words aloud. (I am not claiming I don't say anything to make matters worse, I just don't say these particular words)

David and I continued our well-rehearsed dance of making matters worse until something began to lift as we drove up a mountain pass. I could feel a laugh wanting to emerge at the ridiculousness of it all. When the laugh began to reach my lips, I couldn't quite stick with it. I pondered how to begin the conversation. I wish I had been "well" enough to simply allow the laugh, but it took a few minutes of negotiating until we were ready to let go.

Then we hugged and cried our frustration—and because we have a great big tool bag, and years of practice, we didn't have to rehash ad nauseam.

Here are some tools from the relationship tool bag that David and I have gathered over our two decades together. I don't claim to always use them, but I do claim that when I do use them, they work!

IDENTIFY EXPECTATIONS

How we do that: First we acknowledge we have expectations, then we figure out what they are, exactly. Then we either consider whether to give them up—or ask each other if we are willing to meet them. For instance: I have an expectation that we take our shoes off when we come into the house. David has agreed to do this, but sometimes forgets. We may bicker for a moment about this if he doesn't want to take his shoes off, but he knows he agreed. Another example: David never agreed to drive at a particular speed limit while I am in the car with him. I can get mad at him all I want, but the bottom line is that my expectation is based on my own decision about how he should be. If he goes faster than I am comfortable with, I can choose to drive, or take my own car—or I can just be quiet. (And for you backseat drivers out there, you know what I mean. He is not endangering us; he is simply driving differently than I would like him to).

STOP KEEPING SCORE
How we do that: Yesterday's argument doesn't have to carry over. We don't bring it into our next dispute. We don't throw things in each other's faces. We complete what needs to be completed and move on.

PRACTICE ACCEPTANCE
How we do that: We practice accepting that we are both human. We all make mistakes. We have our moods, our reactions, our fears—and we will continue to have them.

GIVE UP BEING RIGHT
How we do that: We ask ourselves: How important is my position, really? Is being righteous more important than my relationship? For a moment, it may seem more important, but gradually we regain our senses and realize the relationship is more important.

DON'T WAIT
How we do that: This is a hard one!!! We each attempt to be

the first to let go. The first to say "I am sorry." The first to say, "I love you." We do this out of a sense of honor and not from a place of martyrdom or victimization. (If our motivation is to be superior or "I guess I have to be the one *again*," we are missing the point.)

WHEN YOU FORGIVE, BE GENEROUS

How we do that: We don't forgive partially or hold back. We forgive fully. Forgiveness could be defined as "to give as before." Before we formed all our expectations, opinions, and judgments. Before we were hurt or afraid of being hurt. Before we closed off parts of our hearts. Before we were sure we were right.

We all are capable of a great deal more than we realize. Pope John Paul II forgave his would-be assassin, and Nelson Mandela forgave the prison guards who abused him. These examples represent an almost inconceivable level of forgiveness. Yet most of us are experts in holding on to the small grudges. "I don't like how David snapped at me this morning. He shouldn't talk to me like that..." Or "I don't like that tone my co-worker used..." Imagine what would be possible if we were willing to stop holding grudges, to stop being petty. To stop waiting until we're "ready" to forgive.

Why forgive? Because forgiveness is a gift we give to others and to ourselves. It breaks the chains of anger, fear, and hate that bind us. It lets the past be what it is—the past. It allows us, and those we forgive, to move on. It opens up something new for today and tomorrow. We move from the waiting of resentment to the momentum of a fresh clean space.

Or we can forgive simply for the sake of forgiveness.

> To love oneself is the beginning of a lifelong romance.
>
> —OSCAR WILDE

Clearly our relationship is not always poems and peace. We have our ups and downs—our minor disagreements and our major difficulties. Sometimes what we both want to do is *run*. For a moment, we may even believe life might be better with someone else. Maybe that perfect Prince (or Princess) Charming *is* out there somewhere waiting, yet to be discovered. And then we catch ourselves. We remember who we are. And we return to our love and our commitment—our mutual respect and our choice. As the years pass, issues that used to last a few days or even a week now last (at most) a few hours. When the storm passes, we laugh together at what once seemed so significant. We strive to embrace each other's humanity—and to laugh at ourselves (eventually!), even when it's challenging to do so. Like all of life, we get to learn as we go. David and I have continued to do that. Each time we have a doozy of a fight, I wish it were the last, yet to be human is to occasionally disagree, and to be married a long time is to move through many spaces and places.

The most important thing we can do is to learn to love and accept ourselves. We can get to know ourselves as well as we can, find our likes and dislikes, and spend time alone and learn to enjoy our own company. If we don't enjoy our own company, no one else will. Then we will wait forever to find the love that is right there in front of us: the love for ourselves.

From the space of self-love, we can enter into a relationship and *be* the person with whom we would want a relationship.

So how do we do relationships? We keep it simple. Five of my best friends and I get together regularly, and after some struggles within our group, my friends came up with the following list of objectives to live by:

1. *Go out into the world.*
2. *Create relationships.*
3. *Love unabashedly.*
4. *Make mistakes.*
5. *Look for what needs to be healed.*
6. *Forgive your (and others') humanity.*
7. *Thank God for the process and opportunity.*
8. *Love yourself unabashedly.*
9. *Repeat Steps 1-8 until the day you die.*

Gentle Knock:

Are you still waiting for Prince (or Princess) Charming—even if you are in a relationship?

Do you set your partner up to fail? i.e., do you expect them to meet all your needs, read your mind, fill every need? If your immediate response is a disgruntled "Not me!" are you willing to look again, more carefully, for where you might do this?

What are your back doors?

One of the best pieces of advice I have had in relationships (and this applies whether in one or not) is from my mentor, Bill—and I am now offering it to you. He instructed me to write a detailed description of my ideal partner. Next he said, "Now, go be that!"

The truth is that we can have love even when we are not in a romantic relationship. We can love our friends, family, pets, what we do, and where and how we live. If we believe we are not lovable, we will never find the real love or satisfaction we seek. If we do believe it, we can find fulfillment for ourselves and stop demanding that others fulfill us.

Chapter 6:

I Get by with a Little Help from My Friends

Kindred spirit—the very fabric of you is so familiar. It seems as if we are woven of the same thread.

—LEWIS CARTER

I celebrate my treasure trove of friends. If I were to sing the praises of each of the glorious women in my life, I would never be able to remove my fingers from the keyboard. Ever. One of the many gifts of being in Twelve-Step recovery is the depth of relationships that are formed. When survivors of a common peril come together, a bond is formed that is never forgotten. Of course, it's up to us to nurture that bond. And nurture I have. My friends are indeed woven from the same thread—whether we met in Twelve-Step rooms or not. We carry each other through the ups and downs and twists and turns of life. Especially since the fire, my friends pulled me forward when all I wanted to do was stop.

In the months after our house burned down, I gained a whole new appreciation of friendship and the dynamics of giving and receiving. Receiving help from people over a prolonged time of trouble can get very interesting for human beings. To be on the receiving end of love and support over time can challenge even the most balanced of us. Our first tendency is usually to wait until we feel better before reaching out. This is so common that it might be the biggest "waiting" we do when it comes to relationships.

Not long after the fire, I dreamt that I had made one too many requests of my friends, which culminated in being shunned by my women's group. Upon discovering this, all I wanted to do was go home and slam the door. But I knew I didn't have a home. And, suddenly, I was alone.

I woke up sweating. I knew it was my fear surfacing. I knew it was my concern that I would eventually overwhelm others with my requests and need for support. I am not alone in my discomfort with asking for help. Most people are better at giving than at receiving. We struggle to ask. We don't want to bother or burden people. We are afraid of appearing needy. Often we experience ourselves as powerful when we can offer love and support to others, but we don't do quite as well when we are the ones who need to be cared for.

For so many of my early years, when faced with any life stressor, I would retreat and isolate. As it's said around Twelve-Step rooms, "We solve the loneliness problem by isolating." Here's what it looks like: When we are feeling strong and good, we are happy to be with other people. When we are feeling crappy or vulnerable, we wait to feel better before we can bear to expose ourselves to interaction with almost anyone. We isolate and wait for improvement, rather than accept help from those who are only too willing to give it.

Fortunately, by this point in my life, and dealing with this level of crisis, I knew I needed to run towards people, not away from them. I knew that I needed my friends, perhaps more than ever before, regardless of my concerns.

We stayed in friends' basements, borrowed houses, and then returned back to basements again. Our friends brought us food, slept over, helped with insurance paperwork, sifted through ashes where our home once was—and, even more importantly, let us slobber on their shoulders—over and over and over again.

Off and on we stayed at my friend Jessica's. Her entire family welcomed us with open arms and hearts coupled with a genuine invitation to stay as long as we needed. Hmm. A year? How does a year sound, Jessica? I loved it there. I loved being in the metaphorical bosom of one of my best and dearest friends in the whole wide world. Jessica is a rock. Bottom line: Jessica is one of those people that I am not sure I could live—or would want to live—without. In the interest of true friend love, we made a "no leaving" clause early on in our relationship, so we have liberty to unmask our dark sides with each other.

There is great freedom that comes with not having to "behave." So often in life we are overly concerned with what people will think of us. We try to be good, kind, friendly, and polite—and we can drown in that soup of nice. We wait and wait and wait to finally be ourselves, craving to experience the freedom of authentic self-expression, yet we never do if we don't let the messy come out as well.

Jessica and I have allowed a richer experience. We get in fights (not frequently but, when they happen, they seem ferocious). We are both strong-willed women with passionate convictions. At some point (pre-fire) she decided for some odd reason that I was drifting from her, and my startled response was an f-bomb diatribe to rival any rowdy sailor's. Translation: "I am not going anywhere, I adore you, I need you, I am never leaving this friendship, you are stuck with me forever, don't ever doubt it, OK?" It came out a little differently than that, but after my rant, I felt relief—that kind of deep relief that you only can feel when you tell the ultimate truth. I then marched up to her house completely able to give her a more ear-friendly version. (This may not, initially, seem like your cup of tea, but I would suggest not knocking it 'til you try it.)

Having to "behave" is confining. I am certainly not suggesting that we go around dropping the f-bomb at will, or that we give up common courtesy. But there is a certain freedom in friendships where you can show your soft underbelly and your own special down-and-dirty brand of humanity.

Fortunately, I have cultivated this kind of friendship with my peeps. When I count my blessings, I count my friendships twice. Perhaps more than any other area of my life, in my friendships is where I wait the least. I'm a chronic "waiter," so waiting is not entirely absent in my friendships, but I learned early that to have dear friends was not to wait alone. In order to have the kinds of friends you know will be there through thick and thin, we have to go through thick and thin. At some point, we have to stop waiting for this type of freedom and do the work to cultivate it. And the only way this can happen is if we take risks with those in our lives. Stop telling your friends you are "fine" when you aren't. Tell them the truth. Let yourself get messy!

A common trap for many of us is to wait for that one person who will meet all of our needs. We do this in romantic relationships and we do this in friendships as well. Even the best of the best can't meet all of our needs all of the time. Many of us over-achievers know what it's like to try to do that for others. It's exhausting. We need to have multiple names on speed dial. It's OK if there are only a few, but know that you might need to keep dialing when the going gets tough. In the months after the fire, I encouraged those in my inner circle to support each other in their support of me. I know it was draining to be with me sometimes (a lot). My wise friends took good care of themselves and reached out for their own support.

We have walked through thick and thin together, and we *absolutely* know (even when we forget temporarily) that we will be there for each other forever. Yes, I know I keep talking about the lack of guarantees in life but this is one thing of which I am absolutely sure! We also know we will hear the truth from our friends. In the months after the fire, as the stress began to rub us ragged, our friends gave up the niceties and simply told us we looked like hell, then grabbed us in bear hugs.

Gentle Knock:

Whom in your life can you depend on to wrap you in a bear hug? Who has been there to pick you up when your life seems to fall apart? Who is the reliable friend, the one who coaches you the best and never pulls any punches in telling it like it is? Whom can you not see for years and yet pick up where you left off? Are you willing to get messy with your friends?

If you are reading these questions and feeling friendship-deprived, look at qualities you admire in a selection of people you interact with regularly (e.g., colleagues, baristas, fellow committee members, etc.). The truth is you DO have people in your life. What qualities do you admire, and whom might you be willing to call a friend?

Bethany, a hip thirty-something shared this story:

I was always someone who had lots of friends, but what I realized after going through a breakup with my boyfriend and crying alone for weeks on end is that I only felt comfortable supporting my friends and not asking for support myself. I didn't want them to see me vulnerable, yet wondered why I didn't get the comfort I craved. Suddenly, it hit me like a ton of bricks. My mother always said, "you make friends by being a friend," and I had taken this to an extreme! I wasn't asking for support— at all! And, when I realized that, instead of wanting to ask, I wanted to run.

Knowing I was still at some deep level "waiting" for the experience of having a best friend, I decided to take a risk. I felt so alone from my breakup, and I was desperate. I called the friend I had known the longest, and confided my fears to her. She responded in the best way possible, telling me how much she loved and admired me, yet how she had always wanted to be closer but didn't think I wanted to let her in. In that moment, our friendship altered completely, and I slowly got the courage to share myself with other friends as well.

Bethany's story can help us remember that both very friendly people and very shy, reserved, or introverted people often suffer from feeling unsupported or alone. What can we learn about universal themes in how we all wait in friendships?

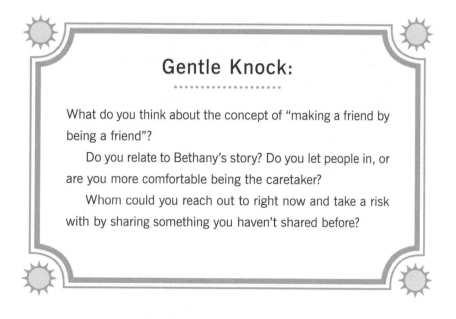

Gentle Knock:

What do you think about the concept of "making a friend by being a friend"?

Do you relate to Bethany's story? Do you let people in, or are you more comfortable being the caretaker?

Whom could you reach out to right now and take a risk with by sharing something you haven't shared before?

This type of messy humanity isn't everyone's idea of the Best Thing Ever. Some prefer relationships to be neat and tidy. Others like them empowered and transformed all the time. I am all in favor of feeling empowered yet, like any good human, continue to have my triggers.

For example. I had an argument with an old friend recently. It came swiftly from an old place in a well-rutted relationship. We both have our roles we play, and we both predictably, in times of stress or strain, torment the crap out of each other. It seems like we "should" be able to get along. We are both great people, yet we often come from very different places, which seem like opposite opinions. (And, they aren't really that opposite, it just ends up that way.) Two wills, not hearing each other in the least, attempting to say what we need to say, but no real messages are received. We end up frustrated, having gathered more "evidence" for our opinion about who and how the other is. The dance we unconsciously choose is the same dance we always do—and after stomping all over each other's toes, we complain to anyone who will listen. Yuck!

This is one of those relationships where I often find myself "wishing" it were different. I wait for this person to change into a more Kristen-approved version of herself. And I wait for me to be different, to be a less triggered, less reactive version of Kristen. It seems like she and I should be the best of friends. For many years, I was heartbroken about this (which is an oh-so-attractive way to be with another). I have had seriously wonderful times with this person, sharing deep, familiar laughter that only a longtime relationship can produce. And I get over-the-top hooked beyond belief when we have our "little" altercations. I let these interactions take me south into obsessive-land, replaying our altercation over and over again. (Did I mention over and over and over again?) All the while hoping for resolution to occur solo in my noggin, which, as you may already be aware, isn't the best place to seek resolution.

What can we do instead in these types of relationships? What other choices can we make?

After one such frustrating conversation, I had the opportunity to go to a Michael Franti concert. Outdoors in the Colorado sunshine, I wondered what would Michael have to say about it all. As his voice filled the stadium, I became convinced he would understand. He would say that love is all that matters. He also would get the darkness, the angst, and, as I watched how he loved on his audience, I figured he would probably give me a big, sweaty bear hug and a peck on the cheek. Then he would write some lyrics. As I write my own "lyrics" in this book, I wonder: Can I let go enough to let love be the thing that shows up? Can I let go of my hurt feelings and my ongoing dilemma of feeling misunderstood in this relationship? Will I? How will it look if I do?

Before I answer that for you, I want you to consider the person who's currently rooting around under your skin. Perhaps you haven't had an out-and-out altercation recently, but chances are there's someone who's refusing to believe or behave as you think he or she should. Chances are good that you will also continue to relate to this person in the same disappointing ways as you continue to wait for it all to somehow get better.

As I channeled Michael Franti in the sunshine, I felt some peace begin to surface. I realized that I could let go of my expectations about this relationship. And I could let go of the fact that I would probably have to let go again. As my mother once said, in some relationships it's like going to the hardware store for peaches. No matter how many times we return to the store, they will never have peaches. It's not what they do. So who was the crazy one for continuing to go back and expecting things to be different? Me.

Then I thanked the good lord above, most recently manifested in the visage of Michael Franti, that I have lots of peeps around me who preach the same gospel. We want the real deal. We want to be heard and listened to in our angst and darkness and messy humanity.

If we have put some care and love and attention into cherishing and deepening our friendships, then we have a good chance of some cushion when it comes to being real and fully self-expressed—which includes the nasty as well as the pretty.

Shortly after the fire, I wrote this to my friends, in gratitude for their love and support:

I will catch you when you are falling. Then you will catch me. Then I will catch you. We will catch each other. We will hold each other. Without you in this world, I don't really want to stay. I may want to vaporize without that type of love and support. Don't tell me that I would be OK without it. I still have my attachments. Most of them burned up, but some I still keep. And I am most definitely attached to YOU! I love your soft and fragile heart, as you love mine. Together we will stand in this fire called life. We will burn up together, and we will emerge like the Phoenix and dance in this crazy, wild world.

Gentle Knock:

What are you, dear reader, waiting to say to your people that needs to be said? What do you need to hear from them? What do you need or want to see from them? How have you made that need clear, or possibly hidden it away like a shameful secret?

Are you willing to ask what they might need/want from you that they might not be getting? You, of course, are free to accept or decline or negotiate a different offer!

So I will cry again when I need to. I will slobber and drool on my dear friends' chests (and I thank them in advance). I will shake and sob. I will giggle in the mix, too. We will walk through this thing called life together. The raw and the beautiful. The wild and the wooly. The deep and the brave. When we have those we call dear friends, we can in fact face all life has to offer, together.

Chapter 7:

She's a Bad Mama Jama

Children begin by loving their parents; as they grow older they judge them; sometimes they forgive them.

— OSCAR WILDE

In a perfect world, as we grow older, our relationship with our parents grows with us. Yet many of us are still waiting for our parents to become perfect or for them to finally accept us. Even though we look like grownups on the outside, often our relationship with our parents is stuck in a time warp. In any uncomfortable interaction, we revert to being a teenager (or perhaps a two-year-old in a tantrum). We can't ever quite see our parents as the people they are—but our main complaint is they don't see us in that way.

Let's start with mom. Mom, the most physically close relationship we will ever have. Mom, whose substance nurtured us in utero, from whose body we were fed. Mom, whom we wanted to be just like or nothing like. Mom, who we fought with, adored, worshiped or reviled. That mom. We have an idealized vision of mom (no matter how ideal our "real" mom might have been) and she is the one we are waiting for, the one whose understanding, acceptance, approval, so often lurks just out of reach. Until we get some clarity and space in this relationship (even if just in our own experience of it), how could we not be waiting, ad infinitum, in so many other areas of life? How could we not be waiting and needing so many other people to approve, only to find out all their approval (if we get it) doesn't seem to make up for this early actual or perceived lack?

BEAUTIFUL MOTHERS

As I consider how we wait to be OK with our mothers, I consider my dear friends Jessica and Dusty, extraordinary mothers both. I watch them with their girl-pairs and learn more about what it means to love. Their daughters are in different stages of life—Jessica's girls three and five, Dusty's ten and almost sixteen. They are all exceptionally beautiful girls, being raised by mothers who are self-aware, strong, passionate, bold, and fiercely loving. These girls have the foundation to become self-assured, bold women in ways that many of us had to learn and earn all on our own through trials and tribulations. Of course, there are no guarantees, but at opportune moments I will remind these girls of who they are and where they come from. I plan on being in their lives for a very long time.

I was fortunate to have my own strong-willed, beautiful, brilliant, and talented mother who is way too far away from me right now in sunny central Florida. Taking my own advice to heart, I stop for a moment to write her these words:

> *Thank you, Momma, for influencing me with a love of horses, hugs, beautiful art, dancing, laughter, and much, much more. You are a beautiful soul and I am glad you didn't give up on having children after your earlier heartbreaking miscarriages. I am grateful to have you as my mother, my teacher, and my friend.*

My mom was a belly dancer, an artist, and a wild-child in the 1970s, and now in her own seventies she still is all of the above, in many ways. I had an opportunity to flash to the past with something that my mom loved to do, while attending a dear friend's belly dancing show in our little mountain community. On a glorious misty, rainy, and chilly Saturday evening, we were bathed in soft light from the stage as countless dancers expressed the beauty of womanhood in all shapes and sizes. The colors were rich, the moves exotic, the beauty real. I could see my mom as one of these dancers, excited, nervous—and willing to let herself be free on stage and move with the music and her troupe. For a moment, I glimpsed my mother as a woman instead of just my mother.

It is a rare and precious moment when we get out of ourselves long enough to catch glimpses of other people as they are— outside of their relationship to us. Whether it's our parent, child, husband, or best friend, we have patterns of relating to them that limit our actually seeing them in their entirety. Most of the time we are on autopilot, business as usual. We rarely have a single second of life when that person is not that role for us. You will have an opportunity to explore this in your own relationships now.

Let's start with your mom. She may have been the most dreadful mother on earth. She may have abandoned you when you were young, or beat you throughout your life. Or she may have blamed you for her angst about the world. Making peace doesn't mean you have tea together on Saturdays. It doesn't mean you even like her. It means you make peace. You find a place in your heart where you can forgive. You find that she was just a human being responding to the world in the way she responded—right or wrong. She once had her hopes, dreams, and aspirations just like you. She didn't plan to be that abuser/ alcoholic/abandoner or simply that controlling person that she became. None of us set out to become that way.

Just as you have had dreams you hold or once held, or dreams that have come true, can you consider that your mom once had dreams too? Possibly the level of her bitterness is directly proportional to how early or dramatically that light got extinguished for her. Perhaps it was circumstances for her. Perhaps she had the same upbringing (or some version of it) that she delivered to you. Maybe you will never know, maybe you already do know, and maybe you will now be able to ask her and to genuinely care.

If the extremes of this don't seem to apply to you, I invite you to look deeper. My assertion is that most of us still have something we could let go of with our mothers. If you really say you don't, look to some other important, impactful person in your life. Perhaps someone who reminds you of your mother... How about forgiving them? Make peace with that person.

Gentle Knock:

For a moment, step out of your relationship with your mother as best you can. Think of who she was as a child, what was her upbringing like, what did she love to do? Imagine you were a stranger observing her life. What might you be able to see about your mother that you haven't seen before? What are you waiting for in your relationship with your mother?

What issues are not healed?

What is your idea of the perfect mother? Could anyone really be that?

LET'S NOT FORGET THE FATHERS

And now a word about dads. He was the first male figure to turn his attention to us, and we bathed in the light of his love. We hoped to follow in his footsteps as we marched in his shoes around the house. We lingered in the smell of aftershave that he left on our cheeks as he kissed us goodbye. We rubbed his whiskered face and peppered him with questions about the world. We tuned in to the base tones in his voice as they etched permanent music in our hearts. Dad showed us what it meant to be strong. He demonstrated bravery, courage, and chivalry. We learned how to relate to other men as we grew under his tutelage. We learned about the masculine side of love.

If it didn't go well with dad, or went only marginally well, we were left with confusion and sometimes chaos in relationships. Just like moms, dads run the gamut from wonderful to horrific. And sometimes they are a little of both.

I have been blessed to know many great fathers. Starting with my dad, who brings wit, intelligence, and the ability to see the richness and depth of the world. Who allows the troubles that exist to break his heart and form his soul. Who is able to love deeply and still be strong. Who is funny and warm to all of those he meets. My stepfather, who loves us like the children he never had, who calls me out of the blue to offer a solution (or two) about something that is troubling me. Who loves my mom the way she has always wanted to be loved. Who is smart and funny—and has a twinkly rebellious streak, too. My brother, who is big, brawny, and brave, yet lets his heart crack open cavernously with his two beloved boys. He tosses them in the air and hopes they will find their wings to fly in the future. He knows the struggles he has faced in his life and wishes those boys could be spared any pain. He constantly strives to be a better dad—yet, in his striving, he already is.

And, then I watch the husbands of my best friends father their pairs of girls. I see heartbreaking love so great and patience so vast it catches my breath. I observe private moments, the brushing of fine hair into pigtails, puzzling with a homework quandary, or tucking these precious souls in bed for the night with vows to protect them from anything ever that might come to harm them. I watch them weep with concern as they watch their girls fall to the ground, fall in love, and have their hearts broken, and still laugh uproariously at their spicy antics. Fatherhood. It's ALL of it. These fathers won't do it perfectly, yet they are perfect *because* they do it.

To stop waiting for perfection in our relationship with our parents means we all need to evolve in the way we relate. Creating and maintaining a mature bond is a challenge. And some patterns may never completely change. My mom still tells me to "be careful" as we hang up the phone no matter what it is I am doing next (even getting into bed to go to sleep), and she still compulsively corrects my grammar and absolutely despises dangling prepositions. My dad, on the other hand, always reminds me to keep both hands on the wheel even when I have removed my hand for a millisecond to straighten a loose hair that has blown in my face.

Gentle Knock:

It's time to answer the same questions about your dad that you did about your mom. Refer back to that list. Take some time.

Now, having done that, it's time to write a letter. Write a letter to both your mother and your father, or pick whomever you had a harder time with growing up and feeling accepted by. Write this letter from them to you, telling you how much they loved you and what they loved about you.

Tabitha, a successful entrepreneur with two teenage boys, tells of her struggles with being a parent:

> *My parents never got divorced—and in many ways I wished they had. They fought constantly, and my brother and I were somehow always in the middle. My parents each chose their "favorite" child and expected us to take their side. When these fights would*

break out, our house turned into a war zone. Nothing was safe, there were mental land-mines everywhere, and no one was willing to surrender. When I finally left the house at eighteen, I promised never to be like them if I ever had kids (which I thought I never would because I was sure I would screw them up anyway!). Fast-forward twenty-five years. I am happily married, with two boys, aged seventeen and thirteen. Yes, over the years I changed and decided to have kids, but what didn't change was my fear of being like my parents. My mom died ten years ago, and I am sad to say we never made peace. I left the house angry and was never able to forgive her while she was still alive. I talk to my dad weekly and even though I was his "favorite" and always took his side, it's as if we can't forgive ourselves for that behavior with mom. We never talked about it, so it has become the proverbial elephant in the room. What scared me into getting some help was that I started to pit my younger son against my husband and my older son. At first this began gradu-ally as a hope that my son would comfort me after a fight. This thought in itself freaked me out! How could I be so grossly awful? Then I began confiding in my son after a fight. Thank God, I was repulsed by my behavior and saw the schism that was beginning in my house. A dear friend and confidant recommended a workshop she had attended and, thankfully, I was ready and willing.

On the second day of the workshop, my grief about my mom's death and my lack of forgiveness came rushing to the surface. I spent the afternoon weeping. Later on, with the encouragement of the workshop leader, I called my dad, and we had the first open conversation we had had in years. We were able to speak the unspeakable about our guilt about the pattern. My dad wept and apologized for putting me in this scenario. I told him what I was doing to my own son.

The harder call was to my husband to cop to what I had started to do. Then even harder than that was talking to both my sons about my behavior. What came from all of this after a lot of tears and difficult conversations was permission for us all to have our old issues and triggers but a new level of awareness of when we're doing it. Miraculously, this dynamic has become something we laugh about instead of getting all serious about. One family member will bugle the battle cry (da-da-da-daaaaaaaah) when I am starting this pattern and we will all laugh (sometimes I am the slowest to crack a smile, but it does remind me to recognize what I am doing). My dad and I have gotten back on track, and now I have also been talking to my brother, who was my mortal enemy growing up. I am not saying it's easy, but we are all breaking the old patterns and creating new relationships.

As Tabitha finished telling me her story we spent some time talking about all the ways we "wait" in terms of forgiving and loving our parents along with the multitude of ways we deny this same love and acceptance to ourselves as adults. Tabitha shared that the hardest person to forgive in all of this has been herself. But then she constantly reminds herself of the importance of self-forgiveness, knowing that if she doesn't do this for herself, on one level she is continuing the pattern.

As you take the time to examine your own patterns with your parents around what you still hold on to and what you haven't forgiven, just for today consider letting go, even on a small scale, of some of that old hurt. If we wait to have perfect parents, or to be perfect parents, we will, in fact, wait forever.

Chapter 8:

Waiting to Become the Person my Dog THINKS I Am

My ambition in life is to someday be the person my dog thinks I am.

— EMILY MAUGHAN

A doration doesn't begin to describe it. Heart-wrenching love, the likes of which I have never felt before, is more like it. I am talking about the love I have for my dogs. Sitting in my writing perch, I have one faithful companion at my feet and another ninety-pound puppy snuggled so close to me on the couch that I almost can't move my hands to type. Do I ask him to move? No. Instead I bask in the love I feel, fed by his love for me, fueled for the moment in my solo journey of being a writer. Later on, the basking continues as I return to the ultimate in learning opportunities: if the gigantic, muddy paw print in the middle of my freshly printed manuscript doesn't remind me of the simple perfection of life, I am off base. *Way off base!*

My husband and I share our lives with two Rhodesian Ridgebacks and one ornery tabby cat. Our animals are often my greatest teachers—they are my "significance barometer." They assist me in seeing when I am off track, when I take life a little too seriously, or when I have forgotten the joy of the moment. They show me the profound gift of the simple things in life. And, when I forget, my animals remind me of who I am.

Animals can inspire us to be less busy, more present, less worried, more joyful, and more passionate about life. They will never judge us for the things we do or don't do. Animals don't complain. They don't create drama. Their type of waiting, healthy waiting, is patience personified. Their view of the world is immediate. While I procrastinate, get stopped by fear, lose sight of my dreams, and doubt myself, my dog Tigger doesn't wait to live. Instead, he leaps with joy onto any bed or couch in sight and is a constant reminder for me to stop and smell the puppy breath. Not content to be ignored, a giant meat hook of a paw will land on my arm or leg if my attention wavers too far. Just now, he raises an eyebrow as he catches me singing his praises. Tigger reminds me to feel excited about the little things; the simple pleasures in life. How is it that dried dog food for dinner (again) never seems to lose its magic? And, another W-A-L-K? Well, that is just plain ecstasy.

Right now, to continue my practice of "not waiting," I drop everything to kiss his sweet-smelling head. That's when I know I am practicing right living: my willingness to stop in the moment and remember what really matters.

My husband, David, and I got our first reminder of what matters in the form of Jaxson, a precious seven-week-old Rhodesian Ridgeback, who quickly became a wild-man, had us question our sanity on a regular basis, then left our hearts in tatters when he died suddenly at eleven-and-a-half years old.

When Jaxson died, my pain was gargantuan, choking out any light. I was traveling when David called with the news. Six months earlier, Jaxson had had surgery to remove a mass on his spleen. After the surgery, the symptoms that had perplexed the doctors for months were gone, and he regained some puppy spirit. Then one night David returned home to find him collapsed on the floor. On the way to the emergency vet, Jaxson stopped breathing. More than three years later, I still weep at the loss of that great dog. I pause to bargain with God or whoever is up there listening: *You better not take Tigger.* Sounds more like a threat than a "bargain," but I mean it. What would I do to follow up on my threat? I have no idea, but it gives me an illusion of control. "Don't you dare. You hear me, Dude?"

Yes, we know they will die one day. We don't want it to happen. We would do anything to stop it from happening. When it does, we mourn deeply. But the thought of another swift shift of life is almost too much to bear. Tigger is only two-and-a-half, but can I keep him safe from the dangers of the world? Yes, I realize this is the question parents have to face every day. We childless pet people know this angst only through soft puppy (or kitty) eyes. Animals trust us. True, their ancestors survived in the wild for eons before humans got involved, but domesticated animals have lost their street smarts. They eat what they find, and sometimes it isn't good. My dogs wander too far and could end up lost to fend for themselves. We have promised to care for them and keep them protected. They protect us in return—and promise to squash our hearts in the process, their lives being so much shorter than our own.

Would I sacrifice this love in order to avoid the heartbreak? No. I am a dog person. Always have been, always will be. They are all beloved. Yet some in particular become our soul mates.

A dear friend, Renata, tells her own version of "puppy love":

> *After losing my mom to cancer, and feeling so utterly alone in the world, I decided to*

*carry on my mother's tradition of adopting
an animal from the local shelter. One rainy
day, I wandered past the cages of the sometimes wagging, sometimes cowering rows of
homeless dogs. My heart ached, as I knew
I could only choose one. How could I ever
choose? I had almost given up hope of making
the "right" choice when one particularly
pitiful sight caught my attention. Blind in
one eye, this creature stumbled to the gate as
I approached. His hair was uneven, his ribs
protruded, one ear stood up and the other
flopped down. He grunted as he moved, but
that tail kept thumping. Something in his one
good eye spoke to something in my searching
gaze. "So, it's you," I thought.*

*Ralph came home with me the next day.
I am not saying it was easy. We went through
a difficult period of adjustment. Ralph was as
stuck in his ways as I was in mine. His good
eye kept getting infected, and for a while we
were unsure if he would retain his sight at all.
Yet, even on the days of wondering just what
I had gotten myself into, some niggling lesson
seemed to be arising. I had been single for so*

long, had only a few close friends whom I almost never saw, was in a job that I was good at but didn't love—and I found myself talking to Ralph incessantly. I would cry about losing my mother, moan about being alone, complain about my job, and Ralph would look at me with his one good eye and thump his tail. If I was silent for too long, it was almost as if Ralph was saying, "OK, it's time to process. I want to know what you are feeling. Talk to me!" as he nudged my arm to get my attention. Then I would start talking, and that tail would go again. I also began observing how courageous Ralph was. Even when he couldn't see, he would run around the house chasing balls, often banging into things. Miraculously, this never seemed to deter him. He would shake his head and keep moving.

Even during extensive vet visits when they poked and prodded at his remaining eye, he would always thump his tail with the patience of a saint. With Ralph, my heart began to open in a way it never had before. I started talking to my friends more, and my friendships blossomed. Then, one day at the vet, a nice-looking man paid a lot of attention to Ralph—and perhaps a little to me as well, as he asked for my phone number. I hadn't been out on a date in years, so I am not sure where it's going to go. But what Ralph keeps teaching me over and over again is to keep my heart open, to keep going for it, even if I bump into furniture and fall down—and to stop waiting to love.

Gentle Knock:

If you are currently an animal owner, what do you think your critter might tell you about your daily choices in terms of how you spend your time, your mood, and your energy?

What do you feel free to say or do around your dog, cat or other pet that you don't say or do around people?

If you don't currently have a pet, what benefit would it be for you to spend some time with animals? And how might you do that?

Sometimes human puppies are the best at helping us see the blessings of our animals. One post-fire morning while my homeless husband and I were living at my friend Jessica's, her five-year-old human angel, Cassidy, peeked over my hands as I wrote. Afraid that the dark and pain-filled words I typed would taint her innocence, I stopped. Then I welcomed the interruption, allowing my heart to open as I listened to her running commentary on all things great and small. "Did you know dogs can paint...? I met a dog named Captain... How old are you?" She tucked Tigger in a blanket as he lay on my feet and kissed his head, exclaiming, "You have the best puppies ever."

With those words, all my troubles stopped for a moment. "Yes," I said, that's true. I have the best puppies ever."

I attribute a large amount of the "sanity" I maintained after the fire to my animals. My love for them, the focus on their well-being provided an opportunity to get out of myself and into their worlds. They know who I am. And I know who they are. There is no waiting to be OK here. There is only being.

As childless people, David and I treat our dogs as our children. Their well-being is of the utmost importance. Even in the midst of our displacement over the summer, Roscoe, the "good one," slept on his dog bed, played nicely with others, did his business in the small courtyard which became their new yard in our temporary home. Tigger pulled like a draft horse, crouching his mass of muscle low to the ground, wouldn't use the courtyard (so required a walk for all of his business). He meandered instead of eating his meals and jumped up on couches and beds everywhere, which didn't always go over well depending on whose home was our temporary landing place.

As time went on, Roscoe continued to adapt well to our vagabond lifestyle. Whereas Tigger, the more sensitive soul, had adjustment disorder.

What began as a deep-throated play bark at the dog park became a territorial growl. Always friendly, never a "problem dog," Tigger started picking fights with random dogs. We could never predict just whom he considered to be a threat or why they rubbed his scruff the wrong way; he would simply brawl and a few times left with minor teeth marks. Once upon a time our dogs had had a good chunk of our acreage to roam. After the fire, they moved with us from basement to basement and became "leash" dogs whose only off-leash time was at the dog park.

Was Tigger going through his own mourning? Was he picking up on ours? We pulled closer together as a furry family during our homeless period. Interestingly, when we finally quit being vagabonds and bought a new home in a new town, Tigger's behavior changed. No more fights at the dog park: he returned to being the ninety-pound goofball he had been before. We all breathed a sigh of relief as we settled into our new routine.

What can we learn from these precious souls as we journey through the minefield of life? Often, in the eyes of our animals, we are someone we don't even know. Their devotion is so great that its reality might stun us. Sometimes, if we are lucky, we feel the same for them. This deep, heartbreaking love opens our hearts beyond their original capacity. If we are willing to love this big, our animals will crack our hearts and leave us bleeding. They can also become a place we can learn to love with no waiting whatsoever. Through this opening, we can learn to extend this love and acceptance to ourselves and even to others who don't seem so easy to love.

Chapter 9:

Unwrap Your Own Gifts

The true profession of man is to find his way to himself.

— HERMANN HESSE

Before the fire reduced my old life to smoldering piles— despite my many years as a therapist, coach, and guide—I *still* secretly believed I needed to do more, be more, and achieve more. Even while I implored my clients to be gentle with themselves, I still had a serious case of "not enoughness," which led to driven-ness in my work.

Even after all I had accomplished, on some deep level, it

wasn't enough. Master's degree, yeah, that's good and all, but, well, my school wasn't the best… Published author, well, OK, but I should be a *New York Times* bestseller… Broken through my fears of being on stage in front of hundreds of people, done many great speaking gigs, but why do my hands still sweat? Why is it still so hard?

Blah blah and more blah! The level of acceptance I had was light years away from the deep self-destruction of my early days, yet I still wanted to prove something and get somewhere. The lie that drove me was that an elusive place of arrival would give me the freedom I craved. One day I would get "there" and whoever was keeping score would award my prize for goodness and I could finally stop trying so hard.

Ironically, in the midst of yet another soul-awakening, I got the offer to write this book. A niggling thought surfaced from the reservoirs of my mind. How could I be writing a book on waiting when I was once again questioning my path? The fire stirred embers of questions in many areas of my life—but none perhaps as much as the area of my career. Even though I loved my work, the biggest part of my "letting go of attachments" declaration was directed at the area of career and purpose. It seemed I so quickly moved from loving what I do into trying to prove something, and craving success—which inevitably led to burnout.

So, while not having it all figured out (also known as "in

the process of having pretty much no idea what's going on"!), what is a writer and an author coach to do? Well, we must say "Yes." As I offered up this Yes, I knew it was a Yes to the challenge. Yes to letting go of the past. Yes to reinvention. Yes to the future. Yes to the unknown. Yes to the missed deadlines and severe self-doubt. Yes to the moments of pure clarity. All these yeses would be part of my opportunity to write these words from a new place without driven-ness, a place from my passion. I would be finding my purpose again, as I found my words to write. I would have something to focus on other than my grief, yet I would be able to bring my grief into my writing in order to tell my true story. I was stretching and growing, again.

Any time we stretch ourselves, we may feel like puking much of the time. We may wonder if we are up to the task. We may question everything. *Again. Really? Again? Didn't I already resolve this? Didn't I already master this? Ah, I see. Apparently there is still more to unravel.*

And we bring all of that along for the ride. I am bringing all of it along for this ride.

The fire may have shaken my notions of career to their core, but it cemented my passion for writing. Five days after the fire I started blogging, and over a period of nine months I wrote over a hundred thousand words. This is no small task. Each morning, I would awaken with thoughts bubbling over and turn to my trusty Mac. Sometimes I wrote the pain; other days I wrote about gifts I saw. I processed my way through my angst and grief and as the word count grew I built my confidence as a writer. I let the raw, unedited words come; I let my grief hang out with all its jagged edges and questions. I said things that were hard to speak aloud.

According to many great writers, no one sits down and writes brilliantly the first time. If you are a writer who does, more power to you. For the rest of us, let us take comfort in the wise words of Anne Lamott—author of many books, including many bestsellers, and a former writing instructor. When she was asked about her writing process during an interview, she replied, "There is no fantasy out there. I don't sit down and say, it's so great to be me. I am in the same boat as the rest of you. I sit down at the same time every day. I do it badly, and then I do it again. I have terrible self-esteem and lot of grandiosity—I carve out a small thing I am going to handle and then I do it badly... A horrible, unreadable first draft is the way home."

How terribly true Lamott's words are. "But I am not creative..." was the mantra that ran through my mind as I stared at the blank paper while beginning my first book. I knew what creativity was—and I was certain I didn't have it. Creative talent and artistic ability were reserved for other people. My parents had it: my mother as an exquisitely talented artist—her drawing from age ten of a herd of running horses that hung on our wall was a constant reminder of how I thought I should draw; my father as an art historian and a curator at the Museum of Fine Arts in Boston—our frequent trips to the museum a demonstration of true art.

Each time I would put pen (or crayon) to paper, my rudimentary stick figures depressed me. The verdict: I had no talent.

In college, I studied art history. I could appreciate talent but once again it was clear I didn't possess it. And I avoided writing anything—even thank-you notes—as I could never adequately express my thoughts on paper.

When, out of the blue, inspiration to write that first book appeared, it was an obvious dilemma for my rigid view of my absence of talent! Fortunately, by this time in my life, I had logged hours upon hours of personal development work. I knew I could "feel the fear and do it anyway." I knew how to take action—to move forward even when every molecule in my body told me to stop. And, I knew how to ask for help. Still, I was at a turning point. I had to transform my view of myself as an artist—and as a writer.

The only way I could do this was to write.

Some days I cried and wanted to give up; others I celebrated my courage. I wrote, rewrote, ripped it all up, and started over. I hired editors, changed directions, then changed back. I danced in the moonlight and curled up in a ball on the floor. I told everyone I was writing and then wished I hadn't. I grew, contracted, and then grew again, stretching further than I ever thought possible.

Starting any new project is challenging. Sitting and staring at the blank screen can be horrific. The thoughts of doubt rush to the surface and threaten to block out any inspiration I have ever felt. More proof of what I tell my clients: you can be tucked away in a mountain retreat, by a river, all alone, and still not be inspired to write. There is no perfect time to write. It takes dedication, saying no to some things to say yes to this, willingness to sit through the discomfort, the ability to watch words that bore you show up on the screen and keep typing anyway. "Don't edit as you write" is a mantra. Yet, of course, we perfectionists can't stand that! I attempt to follow my own advice and type away, knowing I can come back. I could add this to my worry list: maybe I am running out of steam with my writing. And I write anyway. Write regardless. Write on. That's what I tell my clients—and I tell myself that too. Over and over again.

At some point in my journey, I began to call myself a writer, and it started to be true. Actually, I fit right in, because most writers (if not all) have horrific committees in their heads telling them they are terrible. There is so much room for angst in this profession.

And, rest assured, many a day of doubt filled my world as I wrote the chapters in this book. To add insult to injury, in writing this chapter I wondered if once again I was going on a wild goose chase searching for my purpose! Or was this my opportunity to once and for all realize just where my purpose resides? Or what if it was a weird thing in the middle of my process that was neither one of these extremes, neither "wild goose chase" nor "once-and-for-all"?

In teasing apart this thing called purpose, it's clear that many people spend their lives searching for purpose, waiting to find *the right* thing to appear. Others don't allow themselves to dream. Some choose careers based on family expectations and actual or perceived pressures from parents and teachers, while still others work in jobs they dislike, abandoning the notion that they could be happy in a career. They compartmentalize their working lives by saying things such as, "It's just a job—I don't need to like it. I can enjoy my time off and wait for retirement."

Just where is this elusive thing called purpose? Is it locked away deep down inside our souls? Or do we get to create it? Do we go along through life and hope that one day it knocks on the door? "Hello, it's me, your Purpose. You have been looking for me all this time and here I am! Let's get started and do some stuff!" Many of us have been waiting for just that miraculous intervention. I know I was for many years.

In my teens, I frequently wondered, "What am I going to be when I grow up?" Concerned that I was supposed to know the answer to this question—it seemed so many of my peers at least had ideas—inevitably, the next question was, "When, exactly, will I grow up?"

Being a grownup never seemed like a good idea. I had felt unsure of myself for so long; why would I want the responsibility that comes with being an adult? Struggling for so long with my studies, battling my demons and addictions, and barely making it through college did not contribute to any sense that I might ever know what I was supposed to do, let alone find my purpose.

Then came two trips to rehab and my life-altering path of recovery. After a few years of focusing on the basics of how to stay sober and eat healthily, I had an epiphany. Not only was I beginning to thrive, I also was fascinated by the field that saved my life. I became determined to help others as I myself had been supported during my struggles with addiction. I returned to school, worked my butt off, and earned a master's degree in mental health counseling. This was the perfect fit as I continued in my own personal exploration into how we tick, why we are the way we are—and how to break out of destructive patterns. To build experience, I spent a few years volunteering, then interned at treatment centers in the field of addiction—and then got my first job as a counselor. Finally, I felt on track, in the groove, living "on purpose"!

Some years later, an unexpected announcement came: the treatment center where I worked was closing its doors. We were all being laid off. "Now what?" I wondered. Everything had seemed so certain, heading in one direction, but here I was at a crossroads (again) forced to consider what to do next. I had thought I was on the right path, but gradually I faced the truth—after years of watching people struggle, then return to their addictions, I was burned out on a very deep level. Even though I loved my work, the years of hearing people's tragic stories had taken its toll. When I interviewed for similar jobs, a sense of exhaustion took over.

Now what was I to do? I realized I was in a place where I had to choose again.

I jumped into other professions, trying them on, searching for a fit. Real estate? No, that wasn't quite it. Massage therapy? Close. Boutique owner? Not so much. Even as I wandered, I continued my studies and exploration in the field of personal development. I attended training courses and workshops. I listened to lectures. I assisted others on their path of self-discovery, but still I didn't know what I wanted to be. Then one day a dear friend recommended Jack Canfield's book *The Success Principles*. I read it eagerly, and for the first time, I did an exhaustive exercise on creating a vision for my life.

Through this powerful exercise, I realized my many careers

and life experiences had helped form who I had become, but that I am so much more than my job. I saw that while there was nothing wrong with being a "jack of all trades," it was (once again) my old familiar tendency to search outside myself for the answers and to wait for my life really, finally to begin.

And I started to accept that "my purpose" was an evolution versus an arrival.

Gentle Knock:

Are you searching for your purpose?

Does purpose always mean "work" or "career"? What else could it mean?

Where do you think it is?

What words/concepts seem important when you think about your purpose or why you might be here?

What values are important to you? What might your values have to do with your purpose?

How has your past prepared you for the work you do today?

Do you have any hobbies, activities, or maybe even secret obsessions that naturally compel and demand your attention? Is there anything in this activity or pleasure that might have something to do with your purpose?

As I wrestled with my own sense of purpose, viewed my burn out, and evaluated where I have been and where I am going, my interview with Judy, a successful entrepreneur in her mid-forties, provided words of wisdom:

> *Throughout high school my parents drilled into my head that I needed to find a steady living. For my twenties and early thirties I did just that. I sold insurance, made good money—and I was bored silly. Yet I thought that this was what I was supposed to be doing. Then I had a major health scare when I was thirty-six, which shook me to my core. Out of work for three months, my job in jeopardy, I searched my soul for what to do. After receiving a clean bill of health, I accepted a different position with my old company. I kept thinking I should be clearer after my near-death experience, yet all I had was confusion. At lunch one day, an old friend told me about a start-up company that aligned with the experience I had during a summer internship in college. I dug out my old journals from that time, looked back over my life experience, and took a leap of faith by quitting my job and working for the start-up.*

Wouldn't it be nice if I could tell you every-thing fell into place after that moment? Hah! Guess what? I hated the new job!

But something miraculous did happen: I broke out of my rut. I decided to go back to school while working at the company, and after building some experience (and some much needed confidence), I opened my own consulting firm. I have essentially designed my own career based on my strengths, personal connections, and passions, versus choosing what appears to be stable. Instead of seeing any of my paths as failure, I see how each job I had gave me valuable skills and understanding. I realized that, as I change, my career will as well. I am not sure whom I was comparing myself to all these years and why I had this unrealistic standard of how things should look. No matter what, I could never measure up to this false standard. My career and purpose are like a breathing entity. They grow and change and expand. Finally, I am allowing new things to emerge versus forcing them. And I am open to what feels right in my heart in the moment versus waiting for a stable feeling of purpose.

With Judy's message playing again in my head, again I loosen my grasp on my purpose, breathe a deep sigh, and allow for what's next.

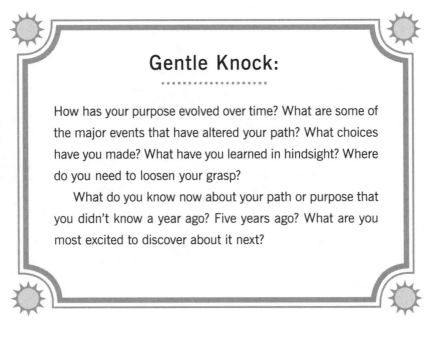

Gentle Knock:

How has your purpose evolved over time? What are some of the major events that have altered your path? What choices have you made? What have you learned in hindsight? Where do you need to loosen your grasp?

What do you know now about your path or purpose that you didn't know a year ago? Five years ago? What are you most excited to discover about it next?

Everything you have ever done has led you to where you are now; everything that lies ahead is an opportunity. None of it is wasted. It's all part of who you are and what you can become. Experience, pleasant or otherwise, provides the ingredients that hone skills, form abilities, and make you special. It's your unique offering to the world.

Now, each day as I sit down to work on this book, I feel an urgency around the fragility of life, all we hold dear; and how life can turn on a dime. As I reevaluate the path I was on and eliminate the irrelevant, I continue to write. It's a strange place to be, to be writing to you and at the same time still working through it for me. In essence, I am inviting us all to return to peace, while acknowledging that we are also going to feel upset and anxious and frustrated some of the time.

When we allow ourselves the space to contemplate our life, our skills, our experiences, our fantasies, and our heart's desire that keeps nagging and nudging us, we find our purpose. The bad news? This call to your purpose isn't going away, but you may not always know how to get from where you are to there. The good news? This call to your purpose isn't going away, so eventually you're going to wind up responding in some way. The only question that remains is how long you'll wait and how you will choose to answer the call when it comes.

Chapter 10:

A Victim of Success

Success is the ability to go from failure to failure with no loss of enthusiasm.

—WINSTON CHURCHILL

The day before my first business trip after the fire, I awoke exhausted and wondered what the hell I was doing. Why was I traveling, why was I leaving my dogs, why was I attending a business seminar, why was I attempting to dress for success from my fire-reduced wardrobe? Feeling off-kilter for much of the day, I headed out to take out the garbage. Seeing a neighbor along the way, I stopped to chat. Hearing the bleep of my phone, I thought, "uh-oh." I glanced down and saw the glaring words of a text "Where are you? We are live on air waiting for you!"

I was scheduled for an interview to talk about my experience hosting my radio show and how this contributed to my greater mission in life. But that was later in the afternoon—or so I thought!

I called immediately. They had been live on air with participants, waiting for me to show up. I had messed up the time zone—the interview had come and gone!

Seeing my spiral of self-flagellation approaching, I apologized as best I could, all the while being stuck in the ten feet of sketchy cell reception where I was. My colleague, Michele, a generous soul and consummate professional, offered to do the interview even though all the participants had already hung up. I gratefully agreed and begged for another delay for me to get back to a clear cell-signal. Those seven minutes were long ones as I admonished myself all the way. How could I have made this mistake??? It had been in my calendar for months... How could I have messed up the time zone? The dark mood of condemnation threatened to take me down.

All I have post-fire is me, I told myself: my reputation, my word, my relationships. Here I was doing serious harm to all of the above. Could I rally in time? How could I have let all these people down? All of Michele's hard work, the other teachers on the tele-seminar, the patient audience coming to learn more about their own self-expression. "Arrrrgggghh-hhhh!" went the not-so-silent scream in my head as I drove the seven minutes back to redemption—or possibly annihilation. Whether I would pull out of my self-inflicted nosedive was up for grabs in those bumpy moments.

When people are generous and others are responsible, miracles can happen. Michele accepted my amends, she was ready to roll. I rallied from down deep inside, and we used this example as a teaching point. We brought authenticity to the interview which would have been there before, but now was so glaring you couldn't miss it. *These things happen.* We don't want them to happen to us, or to be the ones who cause them to happen. And they happen. Since we were discussing radio, it was the perfect segue to talking about how to roll with the punches as you are live on air. The interview was beautiful, and Michele was lovely, and I showed up. I mean that in a deep way. The me that I know myself to be emerged from the funk and fog of wanting to fold and quit. I watched it happen; I felt the scales scrape off as I dragged myself from my earthen cave to face the sun.

One of humanity's greatest strengths is resiliency—the ability to adapt to varied conditions, overcome setbacks, and continue to grow. Even when we doubt this, each of us has this ability; it is our resilience that gets us through the muck time and time and time again. If we stick with "safe," we miss the opportunity to make the necessary mistakes that form the foundation for great success—*whatever success means to you.*

And the real issue is not whether or not we are going to fail, but rather how quickly we can get back up after we fall flat on our faces. What if, as Winston Churchill suggested, we really could get up over and over again with no loss of enthusiasm for our next attempt? Wouldn't that mean that the concept of "failure" has ceased to be so personal and has now just become a thing that sometimes happens and sometimes doesn't?

As a society, we allow external measures to define success. Our social and economic status, the car we drive, the house we live in, our title at work, and the paper quality of our business cards all provide a false sense of meaning. We think of success as an arrival point, a destination we wait to reach. And once we get there, we hope we can stay. We hope to never mess up and jeopardize our arrival. However, this arrival point is often based on an arbitrary set of measurements based on other people's ideas of success that we buy in to. This is the trap. But here's the strange thing: Who, exactly, makes up those "other people"? We do. We are all in some kind of secret agreement society of what success means—and what it doesn't.

On our way to achieving success, many of us decide we have failed before we even begin. Sometimes we believe it will be easier to admit to ourselves that we didn't succeed because we didn't really try. We don't like to think we tried our best but couldn't succeed. Not trying keeps us safe; it protects our fragile egos.

For so long, I didn't set goals because I *knew* I would fail. I had broken so many promises to myself over the years. I would fail an exam and promise myself I would study next time. I would binge and purge and promise to stop. During my addiction, I was incapable of keeping my promises. One day at a time, as I kept choosing recovery, I learned to trust myself to do what I said I would do.

Gentle Knock:

Define success for yourself. What does it mean?

What words/concepts are most important to you when it comes to your truest and most personal version of success?

Are there any parts of your definition that might not belong to you and that you might have borrowed from someone or something else? Are you ready to leave any of those behind? What would it mean for you if you chose to do so?

What does "success" look like for you on the outside—what we'd see if you were on camera—and what does it feel like for you on the inside?

How else can you define success?

My amazing sister-in-law is a marathon runner. She wasn't always this way. As a youngster and into adulthood she trained as a dancer. She was strong and fit but not fast. At one point many, many moons ago, I could kick her butt running. Hah! Never again could I do that. I stopped running, and she passed me long ago. Her first marathon was in 2009 and now she trains in rain, snow, sleet, hail, and well-below-zero temperatures, as she lives in the wilds of Wyoming with my brother and two nephews. Patricia has run marathons on the coast of California and in the woods of the Wild West. She always finishes at the top. She blew her knee out last year and got back into training the moment she could (and probably a bit before the doctors would have approved). Next up for her? A 100-mile trail run. Yes, you read that correctly. That's one hundred miles of running. One hundred miles in a row. Egad! That, I cannot even imagine. I will keep my numbers in word count only.

Yesterday she emailed some photos recently shot for promotion that are beyond amazing. Her six-pack abs showing under her tank top. Action shots with her jumping for joy on the boys' trampoline, running, or simply hanging out on her deck, all the while looking naturally gorgeous. I am quite proud of her. When that woman sets her mind to something, she does it. Plain and simple. No ifs, ands, or buts. Does that mean she never sweats it out in the night, wondering if she is delusional to go for this latest dream? I'm guessing even the iron-abbed Patricia has her dark moments of serious doubt.

The difference is, she doesn't wait for that doubt to go away. She doesn't wait to "get clear" about how she's going to manage this next incredible feat of athleticism. She knows she wants to run and she runs, and in this there is no waiting for success.

We all know how hard it is to stick with a goal that is outside the norm. Regardless of our goal or aspiration—most of us share a predictable tendency toward agitation and agony when we reach for something beyond our current grasp and get confronted with all we risk when we leap instead of wait.

But if we don't try, we cheat ourselves. We don't give ourselves the lessons and experiences it takes to succeed. What will it take for us to realize (and accept) that failure is just a part of the journey and is a necessary component of success? And that while failure might mean something (perhaps just that we need to enjoy some more practice and experience in this area of life), it doesn't usually mean that something has gone wrong, or that we are doing something wrong, or that we are just "wrong" in general and that there is no hope whatsoever.

Gentle Knock:

How would you describe your relationship to "failure"? What is a "failure" as far as you're concerned? Do you tend to treat it as something temporary that requires adjustment or as something permanent that means something bad about you or others?

In which areas of your life are you most likely to take your failures too seriously?

When you fail, what do you do next? Do you usually try harder or do you ease off the pedal for a bit? (Neither one of these strategies is right or wrong)

In terms of resilience, what strategies or ideas tend to help you bounce back from "failure"? What ideas tend to keep you stuck?

I didn't like how I felt in messing up my interview time. I don't enjoy making mistakes—nor do I usually celebrate them as part of my path to success. Winston Churchill's quote on success is one of the best I have seen—but I would change it in this way: "Success is the ability to go from failure to failure with only *temporary* losses of enthusiasm."

I lose my enthusiasm from time to time. I forget what matters and what doesn't. I forget that my worth is not measured in externals. I forget that I love what I do when I try too hard to do it. And then I remember again.

What is the answer to the success question? Allowing ourselves freedom. The freedom to be and do. The freedom to experiment and fail and win. It's the freedom to live a life full of adventure and discovery. It's to live big and messy.

Now success is writing a damn good sentence; looking into my husband's blue eyes; or patting my dogs' heads. It feels like the fuzzy wool blanket I carried from the fire, feather pillows, good socks. Its rewards are my Mac computer, a fast Internet connection, a good book, a long nap, and quiet walks in the woods where there are still some green trees with needles that whistle in the wind.

Chapter 11:

Waiting for My Ship to Come In

Money is only a tool. It will take you wherever you wish, but it will not replace you as the driver.

— AYN RAND

Every week I get on the phone with a group of very cool women, and we talk about money. We go beyond simplistic musings in the realm of the subjective; we celebrate the spiritual aspects of abundance, but we also do something much more potentially unsettling. We get down and dirty in the world of objective reality; we talk about cold, hard cash and our relationship to it. We talk about desire versus want, commitment to our dreams and our vision in life, our messed-up relationships with money, what we learned from our parents, our culture, society, religion, politics—every possible iteration of this topic. It never gets old; we never run out of things to say—and, quite often, it's confronting!

On a recent call, we explored our hidden beliefs about money. We allowed ourselves to unabashedly answer the question: "What does money mean to you?" As in what does it *really* mean to you, not what do you think it *should* mean! The variety of responses was illuminating:

Freedom
Danger
Success
Fulfillment
Burden
Guilt
Excitement
Love
Security
Happiness

We went on to explore messages we have heard and absorbed and (sometimes) practiced ourselves regarding money. Again, the answers were across the board:

Spend wisely.
Spoil yourself—no one else will!
Die broke.
Money is scary.
Abundance is everywhere.
Be a millionaire, but don't appear like one.
Debt is terrible.
Invest in your growth.
Don't be greedy.
It's rude to talk about money.

Arguably, more than any other area, we are the most confused about money.

Gentle Knock:

Take a quick look at what money means to you. Don't censor yourself; just write down the words that come to your mind in this moment.

Another take on this exploration is to consider the opposite: What do *you* mean to money? A lot of people have hidden (but massive) inferiority in the face of money—that is, they feel that, in the end, money is the boss, and it's a boss they'll never understand or please, and their lives are therefore insignificant in its shadow. What comes up for you when you ponder this question?

You won't be surprised to learn that losing "everything" (or almost everything) in a fire offers plenty of rich opportunities to reexamine one's relationship to money on a daily basis. Since money is one of the most potent and powerful areas that keeps us waiting, praying, hoping, and—not proud of it, but let's be honest—whining, I hope my story will help shed some light in the dark closets of your money consciousness. And please don't take it personally, because almost all of us have some dust and grime lurking in the corners.

After being a shopper all my life—although a *somewhat* reformed one since I matured in my money beliefs—my closet full of clothes, shoes, and jewelry vanished in a puff of smoke, so to speak. Shopping for fun is one thing. Shopping because you don't have any socks is another. Now, with six pairs of socks to my name and an overall smaller supply of clothes, I realize I wouldn't want those shelves, drawers, and hangers full of clothes anymore. Since the fire removed the majority of what used to be my fabulous wardrobe, I have come to appreciate on a deeper level than ever before that all those choices didn't necessarily make me one bit happier.

Sure, I have my favorite things, still. And I also mourn— with respect and reverence—some of my lost favorite things, like the furry winter boots that kept me toasty throughout the snowy days, and that I always got complimented on, and that I can't buy again because the company went out of business!

I miss those boots, a lot! On the other hand, knowing that I could pack all my clothes in fifteen minutes if I needed to do so is a comforting thought. And the simple truth is that, for most of us clotheshorses, we don't wear all that stuff anyway.

So much for the wardrobe. Sigh. However, you probably won't be surprised to learn that the early days after the fire were ripe with other money triggers just waiting to be tripped. On my first trip to the bank carrying a large reimbursement check from our insurance company (meant to represent "our structure," otherwise known as our precious lost house), I was in for a rude awakening. Into the bank I went, pleased to have finally received this check and ready to have some financial breathing room for our near future. The bank had other ideas. Apparently, the deal was that, even though we continued to pay our mortgage on the nonexistent house, the bank's policy is to keep all the money and dole it out at their predetermined milestones along the way. To add salt to the wound, this was handily tied to other monies that were lumped in with that large check—and that we needed to live on.

In that moment, fear took over, and I was beyond furious. The sympathetic banker who was the unfortunate bearer of the bad news glanced at me kindly. Tears choking out any ability to think, I steamed out of there, calling my husband as I fled.

A total loss of a house is a devastating financial hit for most people; it's another thing entirely if you have a mountain property or anything with acreage. There is little (if any) coverage for damage to the land, not to mention no coverage for loss in property values. A forest full of burned toothpicks is what remained of our once glorious setting.

So yes, I was triggered. The lack of control over our own money brought my fears raging to the surface. Just as I felt helpless on the day I fled from my home, I now despaired for our future. All the work, the courses I had taken, the books I had read, the years spent talking with my Abundance Group flew out the window. I was gripped with dread. "We are ruined," I thought. "If only we had built up a savings account, if only we didn't have debt, if only I made more money, if only..."

When you're in the midst of a triggering fear, it's difficult to remember to breathe, but fortunately the body takes over and breathing happens on its own. After a good shoulder-shaking cry, slowly but surely the fear loosened its grip. With the help of my husband and my friends, I remembered to take it one step at a time. What appeared devastating in that moment might not be as horrific as I thought. We weren't going to starve; we weren't going to be out on the street; we would, in fact, be OK.

When you're looking at your own triggers and stories about money, a good place to start is in your formative years. If you've never articulated the stories about money you absorbed from your parents, family, and friends while you were growing up, you may be surprised to see how many of those narratives rule the roost when it comes to your own experience of having or not having money.

For much of my teenage life, money meant acceptance and an access to fitting in. After my parents' divorce, I moved back and forth between households, frequently changing schools and having to start making friends all over again. Returning to Florida to live with my mother to finish my junior and senior years of high school, I was to attend an exclusive private school, which promised to prepare me for college. All I could think about was wearing the right clothes. With determination, I spent an entire afternoon trying on different outfits. I was sure I'd found the one—light blue striped chinos, a button-down white blouse, and the cutest tan wedge sandals. I pulled into the parking lot in my sparkling white Chevy Chevette, feeling pretty proud.

My first glimpse of the campus included rows of BMWs, Mercedes, and Cadillacs. In the distance were perfectly mani-cured lawns, a fountain, and a bell tower. Was this my new school or an elite country club? As I walked toward the build-ings, cheerleaders talking together turned and laughed. Later I learned their verdict—tacky shoes.

Unfortunately, this wasn't the first time I got the clothes "wrong" when I changed schools. I became convinced that if I could buy the *right* outfits and fit in, everything would finally fall into place, so I begged my mother to give me the credit card and spent hours in the mall picking out new clothes. This behavior followed me into adulthood. Plastic became the answer. Layaway—what does that mean? I couldn't wait, I needed it *now*! I told myself I deserved it as I snuck my shopping bags into the house.

I never learned the value of earning the money to purchase what I wanted. I bought clothes I never wore. I became a bottomless pit—a compulsive shopper who wanted the finer things in life, but didn't believe she could earn the money to pay for them. I was waiting to hit the jackpot, not believing I could create it for myself. I lived the fantasy that it would come from somewhere outside of me, so I didn't have to be responsible. In recovery, I saw that my behavior was rooted in my deep lack of self-worth. Only by deliberate and conscious intervention could I begin changing my deep-seated beliefs and actions.

Our basic needs are actually quite simple: air, food, water, and shelter. We can categorize just about anything else as a "want." Unfortunately, our wants can become a bottomless pit and can run us ragged in pursuit of them. Media and advertising geniuses prey on our insecurities. "Feeling empty inside? Buy this, take this trip, you'll feel better. Try some retail therapy, and you'll be happy."

Many people still believe that "he who dies with the most

toys wins." We may pretend we don't believe that anymore, thinking, "Oh, that's so 1980s," but underneath, we still look for the next hot, "have-to-have-it" thing. We want it all *now*—the newest cell phone, the smallest laptop. No waiting here! We want instant gratification—we want what we want when we want it.

A few years back, on a trip to Los Angeles, I had the pleasure of being introduced to the world of Jimmy Choo. My dear friend's closet was heaven, with rows of beautifully crafted, stunningly gorgeous shoes. (Remember my shoe issue from high school?) Suddenly, my favorite pair of black sandals was *not enough*. I had to have Jimmy Choos! But my budget didn't support this craving. The wheels started turning: How could I get them? Did I have enough room on my credit card? Would my husband notice? The thought pattern felt all too familiar: It begins as a craving, becomes a longing, and then launches an obsession which I disguise as a need. There will be no satisfaction until I have what I want as I spend my way to my imaginary jackpot.

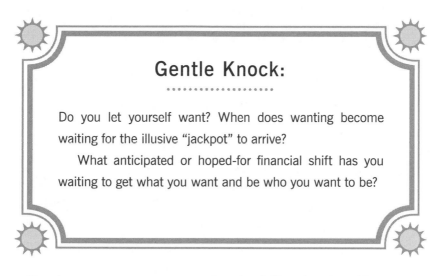

Gentle Knock:

Do you let yourself want? When does wanting become waiting for the illusive "jackpot" to arrive?

What anticipated or hoped-for financial shift has you waiting to get what you want and be who you want to be?

Our ignorance costs us—not just in dollars but in self-esteem too. My friend Joan shares her story:

> *I came from a lower-middle-class family. Both my parents worked hard and provided for us the best they could. Every day after school, I babysat for the neighbors to earn extra money for my family. The school I attended had a lot of rich kids, some of whom were my friends. I didn't want to have my friends over to my house. Their houses were so much more fun. I shared a room with my sister, whereas many of my friends had suites the size of my entire*

house. We would swim in their pools, eat their exquisite food, and play croquet on their lawns. We played dress-up for hours, lost in the vast closets of their mothers, trying on clothes. Many of my friends were generous and let me take home "extra" clothes they didn't wear.

I started to resent the fact that my family couldn't live like this. It didn't seem fair. I vowed to live the way my friends did. Being a good student anyway, I excelled in school, went to the top of my class, and went to law school on loans and a scholarship. After grad- uating from law school and getting a job (with the help of my best friend's parents) at a top law firm, I started making more money each month than my father made in a year. I bought a penthouse apartment, wore the best clothes, and ate at the finest restaurants—only I wasn't happy. So I bought a fancier apartment, a new BMW, went on a trip to the Caribbean, and still I wasn't happy.

I finally realized the money wasn't going to make me happy! I saw I had been ashamed of the way I grew up, embarrassed by my working-class parents. I had been making all

*of it wrong—my family, my friends, myself,
and most of all, the money itself. Coming from
this place, there was no way I could be happy.
After coming to terms with this and apolo-
gizing to my dear family, I realized I could
choose to make money but not be driven by
it. I realized there was nothing wrong with the
money itself. What needed to change was my
attitude towards money.*

Changing old habits isn't easy. I did not act on my impulse that
day in Los Angeles. However, I did continue to want those
Jimmy Choos. In this case, waiting paid off. To celebrate the
completion of my first book, a group of dear friends came
together and bought me my very own pair. Did the shoes make
me complete? No. But did I take pleasure when wearing them?
You betcha!

And, in those crazy moments as I cast around at what
precious items to take as I fled from the fire, I grabbed those
shoes (*after* grabbing my animals) and threw them in the car
before leaving my house for the last time.

Gentle Knock:

What are your triggers around money?

How does waiting to examine your money reality keep you locked in place and frozen in freedom?

What is your money reality? How much do you have in the bank? How much debt do you have? Yes, this can be agitating. But remember, we're talking about Not Waiting here. You don't have to "do" anything about these numbers right now. Just look.

How would you describe your Top Stories when it comes to money—make a list of EVERYTHING that comes up for you (see the list at the beginning of the chapter to get you started) and then divide your stories into "empowering" and "confusing." Look at your beliefs about your own abilities with money and also what you believe about other people who have more or less than you have.

* * *

As if it wasn't challenging enough that our money (or at least, our property and property values) seemed to be burning up and vaporizing into space about as fast as our house dramatically did that spring, an even bigger challenge rose to greet us. There's the money going out—and then there's the money (and love, and gifts, and help) that came pouring in. What were we to do with all this generosity? How could we confront the feelings stirred up by this type of abundance?

Since the fire, our friends (and even strangers) have been sending us money. This was a hard one at first. People kept asking if they could support us financially. During the early days, we declined. Then we saw the pile of rubble that once was our home; and then we read our insurance policy and realized its limitations. We said yes.

We received a sweet five-dollar donation from someone whose name we didn't recognize and couldn't pronounce. Classmates whom we hadn't talked to in years sent us money. A coworker of David's donated. Both a new friend and a very old friend gave us jaw-dropping amounts. We weren't sure how to handle this influx of abundance and generosity. One day, a particularly wise friend admonished: "Shut up and say thank you! What goes around comes around. You would be doing the same thing." I heeded her wise advice. I shut my mouth and kept saying yes.

The willingness to give in life must balance with the willingness to receive.

Yet receiving challenges everything. Even remembering the dollar amounts we received shakes me up a bit. We don't (in our oh-so-polite society) like to talk about money. It is not couth. It is not done. Why are we so awkward about it all? Maybe if we relaxed our tight grip on our views and could peer into others' thoughts, we would realize that everyone gets funny about money. My unexpected trial by fire has altered everything. I am giving up being "proper" around money— and other things as well. If I don't let this fire burn away my old limiting beliefs, then what's the point?

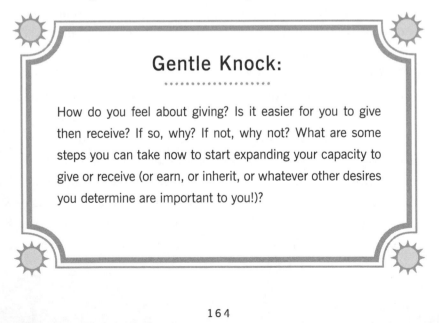

Gentle Knock:

How do you feel about giving? Is it easier for you to give then receive? If so, why? If not, why not? What are some steps you can take now to start expanding your capacity to give or receive (or earn, or inherit, or whatever other desires you determine are important to you!)?

David and I promised to allow this tragedy to remind us how precious life is and how quickly it can shift. At each major turning point of our lives together, we have reset our course, and now our money beliefs have shifted as well. I view this area as a work in progress. Old behaviors can take a long while to change. Baby steps are what have helped in this area. Early in recovery, I realized a closet full of the "right" shoes and clothes wouldn't fix me, yet the tendrils of this old coping mechanism stayed in my psyche for years. Losing that closet full of fabulous clothes to a raging fire quickly left me metaphorically naked, and I was forced to see what remained.

As Billy Idol, one of my favorite rockers from the '80s, said: "It doesn't matter about money; having it, not having it. Or having clothes, or not having them. You're still left alone with yourself in the end."

I couldn't agree more, Billy.

Chapter 12:

Finding True North

A man travels the world over in search of what he needs and returns home to find it.

— GEORGE AUGUSTUS MOORE

Now that we've had a look at our money (an area ripe with waiting, as we've witnessed), it's time to turn our attention to another aspect of our reality that has an immense effect on our happiness and lack thereof. We need to take another look at that place we call home.

After the fire, home has been many things and many places for me and my husband: a 1967 Airstream trailer, a variety of hotel rooms, a couple of dear friend's basements, and then finally a new home in a new neighborhood, still in the mountains, but close enough to a fire station to allow me to sleep at night.

But oh, before the fire. That's a different story. Let me tell you about "home."

Before the fire, home was a little house perched on the side of a mountain with views that went on forever. The morning of the fire I sat drinking my coffee on my favorite leopard-print chaise by the window, one ninety-pound dog curled up at my side, the other at my feet. I gazed at the view, which even after nine years, I never took for granted. "Ah," I thought. "Life in our dream house, our little paradise of a retreat on the side of a mountain. How lucky we are."

I remember the first time we found our home. The ad in the paper sounded too good to be true: thirty-seven acres, two-bedroom, one-bath, far-ranging views—and an exciting bonus: completely "off-the-grid," meaning solar power only. After getting used to mountain living four years earlier, we craved even more adventure. As we walked to the property down the mile-long jeep trail of a road, through groves of shimmering aspen trees, the view began to emerge. Each step we took closer, we held our breaths a little more, fully expecting to be disappointed at the end. We had encountered many near misses in the search for our mountain dream home, finding houses that didn't quite do it, that sounded good on paper yet never felt like *our* place. As we rounded the last corner, we glanced at each other as the sweetest profile of a house I had ever seen greeted us. Set against towering pines and perched on the side of the hill, this sanctuary looked out over a vast expanse of mountain ranges, including Pikes Peak sixty miles to the south.

Each time I pulled in my driveway, I would take a moment to admire that sweet profile of our magical home and breathe a sigh of relief. We had found our forever home, and I was so glad to be home forever.

Two days after the fire, still not knowing the fate of our home, I drove to the fire station. I gave my name and address, and they led me to a bench to sit down. A very nice deputy came in and said it would be a few minutes. My stomach sank, as I had hoped they would send me on my way and tell me not to worry.

Looking back, it reminds me of a scene in the movie *Water for Elephants*. The main character is given the news that his parents have been in an accident. The shot of him walking into the hospital captures a particular mood: those final moments before everything is about to change, when life is still the same but information that you don't want to receive is right around the corner. We want to slow time; we grasp at moments to hold on to.

Here's how my scene looks:

As I sit here waiting to be comforted and dismissed, I study the hallway. A door is propped open with a five-gallon water bottle, a lone lamp stands in the hallway, seemingly out of place, and I sit on a wooden bench tucked against the wall; people walk by and some smile kindly.

Then the lead investigator comes and sits down next to me. I brace myself. He smiles at me gently, then points to my name and address on "the list." In this moment, my life is altered forever.

> *We shape our dwellings, and afterwards our dwellings shape us.*
> —WINSTON CHURCHILL

Home is where the heart is. Home is what you make it. Home is where we lay our head or hang our hats. Home is just another word for you. There are many metaphors for our relationship to home. We sing songs, write poems and capture images of what it means to us.

Home symbolizes warmth, familiarity, a place to recharge, our sanctuary—even love. It's the place we can take our shoes off, take our game face off, and unwind. We can be ourselves, let down our guard, take a deep breath, or sleep the day away.

To say we were "homeless" after the fire is a strong statement, given what that term means in today's world, yet it is also true we were without a home. On a live television interview filmed where our home once stood, I shared the ups and downs, the roller coaster of emotions. I talked about the daunting task of having to list every one of our lost possessions for insurance purposes, the generosity of the community, the rallying together of the neighbors, and the fright of that chaotic day. I sifted through rubble and cried when I picked up charred remains of my granite counter tops and they fell apart in my hands.

David and I soaked up the details while in that house. We fully experienced moments—they were rich, comfortable, safe, and cozy. I loved looking at the colors of the walls, contrasting against other colors. Deep purple in my office, sage green in the hallway. I loved my wooden stairs where dog toenails had scratched a familiar trail. I loved running up the steps to my room, hearing the echoes my feet made as I took three right turns while holding tight to the custom railing that a dear friend hand-crafted for us. I loved the blue-green washed wall in the bathroom that was such a unique combination of colors that we could never match it with touch-up paint. I loved the glint of the stained glass that other friends lovingly crafted for us—a moon and star set against a sky of azure. I loved the handmade barn-wood doors that David meticulously built.

When I fled from my house, I really didn't think it would

be my last time there. My brain clouded with confusion as the cloud of smoke and ash grew closer and closer. My last moments were filled with roaming room to room and staring blindly at most things. After the dogs and cat, a bag of clothes, two of my mother's paintings, some photographs, and our computers were in the car, I would run back in and stare again. In my office, I grabbed my computer monitor but it was bulky, and I was clumsy due to my over-stressed noggin. After I banged it on the wall, then the door frame, I put it back on my desk and left the house again. I returned one last time to grab the dog dishes and food before I turned my back for the last time. It was surreal, a rushed exit, making split-second decisions about what should come into this next phase of our life without knowing that's what I was doing.

Before the fire, I had a recurring nightmare in which we sold our house and, for some reason, I was OK with it until we were past the point where we could turn back or change our minds. Then I completely lost it, coming unhinged. Like a wild animal trying to claw its way out of a cage, I desperately tried everything to stop the transaction or change the plan...to no avail. The next morning, I always awoke heavy-hearted and hung over from this nightmare. That nightmare proved prophetic.

There will always be a line of demarcation: life before the fire and life after the fire. Even now, occasionally, I engage in "I can't believe it." I allow myself to really not believe it. I imagine my home still standing. I see that little house in all its glory and can feel, smell, and hear what it was like to be there. My life is still on the track that it was, and my oasis patiently awaits my return. Just for a moment I indulge. Just for a moment, I want to forget, or return to normal. I want to go back.

The craving for "home" is strong and makes me weep right now. That deep bone-level craving I have been keeping at bay. Home. My want for home, my need for my home, my longing for my home. Even now, in my new home I crave that old home.

Gentle Knock:

Do you experience a longing for a metaphorical or real home you have had? Can you connect the longing for that "home" with a longing for a specific feeling, mood, or self-identity? Perhaps an idea of yourself as safe and at peace? Or the experience of yourself as totally loved and cared for— symbolized by all the color and lushness and loving gifts of friends and family—and utterly protected from the ravening wolves of the Outside World?

For a moment, consider the concept of home as another expression of your true self. Where might you be waiting to experience your true home or self? Or waiting to grieve for a lost home or self? Or waiting to accept a lost home or self?

My home remains a tender memory for me, as tender as the new self that has emerged since the fire. Right before our first site clean-up, I remembered my nightmare of losing my home and descended into the panic that was previously reserved for my dreams. I was well-practiced in changing the thought, meditating or praying, surrounding myself in white light, seeing the gift—but, at that moment, none of these techniques worked worth a damn. A deep panic engulfed me. It threatened to swallow me whole. I had lost my home—it was my nightmare come true.

As we prepared for the site to be demolished, the only thing left of our home at that point was a pile of rubble. But it was still something that had form. I feared that, after the debris was removed, nothing would exist but a memory. Like letting go of a body after a death, I was clinging to something. As the crew arrived I thought, "Oh, please be very gentle, very kind, very loving. Whisper while you work, hold love in your heart." Willing myself to words, I quietly told them, "You will be doing surgery on my heart and what remains of this dream. We will be searching for artifacts to remind us of what once was. Please be gentle." And they were.

WAITING FOR THE CURE...

As I look back on my relationship to homes and my attempts to find myself throughout the years, I recall first hearing the term "geographical cure," in 1989 at a Twelve-Step meeting. I snapped to attention, as it summed up so much of my life up to that point. It refers to the illusion that life will be better when we get *somewhere else.* So we expectantly wait until we get *there* and "there" is somewhere, anywhere other than where we are right now. We think, "I'll be happy when I climb that mountain. When I go to Hawaii. When summer arrives. When I live in that kind of house. When I finally visit that distant country." And, once we get to that place, we hope it will magically change what's wrong in our lives. What we forget—repeatedly—is that we take ourselves and all of our baggage with us wherever we go.

A geographical cure is our "fix" for our problems. By changing where we are, moving our location, or shifting things around, we actually avoid looking inside to the source of our malcontent. Sometimes our problems go away temporarily, but inevitably they return as we find that "we" are still there. What a bummer!

It's true that certain places are magical, wondrous, and desirable. Who doesn't think about their own insignificance when viewing the magnificent expansiveness of the Grand Canyon? Since the beginning of recorded history, religious sages have made pilgrimages to majestic mountaintops to commune with God. Our own country was created as pioneers explored uncharted territories like the western United States with hopes, visions, and dreams of creating something better, which of course drastically altered the concept of "home" and "place" for the people who were already living there—but that's another story.

On the flip side, places do help us see our place in the world, if we let them. Places can help us grow, and learn. In some places, we make new friends, explore our own self-expression, and become the person we always thought we might be. But we can also look at them as one more thing outside ourselves where the answer lies—as was my tendency.

My sister-in-law Patricia shares her geographical adventure.

I love where I live, but it wasn't always this way. My valley (yes, I feel ownership for it in a way that is powerfully connected to all its inhabitants) is a source of support and comfort for me. Every time I return from vacation, I think, "Wow, thank God that I am home." The thankfulness comes not from the dislike of other places, but rather from the comfort of knowing that I choose to create my future anywhere I call home. I grew up in Alaska and felt confined, wanting more than anything to leave and one day be free.

At twenty-three, I finally escaped and found myself sailing for a year and a half down the Intracoastal Waterway to the Bahamas. Money being the deciding factor, I came ashore in Ft. Lauderdale, Florida, only to find myself, six months later, skiing the slopes of Jackson Hole. I felt grounded in Jackson, at home—a feeling that I had never experienced. The Tetons became my higher power, like a motherly source of inspiration—constantly shifting and changing, although really always the same.

In what occurred as a stroke of bad luck, my boyfriend (now husband) needed to go back to Florida to continue his flight training. I reluctantly went with him, even though I desperately wanted to stay in the first place that really seemed like home.

After two years in Florida, two years in Maine, two years in Rhode Island, and two years in Colorado, I returned home to Wyoming. Strangely, my friends were all eight years older! Without the geographical changes and experiences, I would not be the person I am today. I have a master's degree, two amazing children (born in different states), sobriety, and a spiritual completeness that comes from finding myself and coming full circle. It is strange that I had to leave a place to be able to come back.

In the coming back, however, I found who I am.

Often when I travel, I try places on. Sometimes the line between old behavior (the seeking of the geographical cure) and my inquisitiveness is faint. I wonder, "Would I like it better here? What would my life be like? Would I be happier?" I have even gone as far as spending the day with a realtor in some places. Each time I go through this, I see hidden aspects of myself. Sometimes I discover that I am craving change. Sometimes I just don't want to go back to work on Monday. Sometimes I think a *different* set of hills will do the trick. After all the years of personal growth, when we found our mountain home, I settled in a way I never had before. I stopped needing to wonder and wander. With that home lost to fire, without that anchor, who am I now? Am I the same? Am I different? Am I more free? Am I less?

Gentle Knock:

What does home mean to you?

Where have you lost the sense of home? Describe the loss.

Where are the places where you have felt most at home? How did factors of people and atmosphere contribute to that feeling?

What about the places that tempted you to make your home? What elements are seductive, comforting, appealing, exciting to different parts of your being?

My friend Ellen shared a passage she read in a book called *Super Rich* by hip-hop mogul Russell Simmons (the producer of the Beastie Boys and Run DMC). He talks about feeling stifled in Queens, the neighborhood where he grew up. He decides to move to the Lower East Side of Manhattan, during a time when it was an affordable, eclectic, edgy, and extremely exciting neighborhood. He shares about wandering around in wonder at the diversity and contrast—the incredible wealth and poverty, the billion-dollar business deals and the back-alley coke deals and tiny bistros and art dealerships and Hasidic Jews debating in the streets. He writes, "The energy of that neighborhood served as a constant living and breathing reminder that I was part of the world, that the possibilities were infinite, that I wasn't locked out or trapped but rather had the whole world in front of me."

These words encourage us to submerse ourselves (if only for the day) in other interesting neighborhoods. Whether we are willing to try this in reality or only metaphorically, it can allow us to tap into new sources of inspiration and fall less often into old traps of waiting.

I adored my mountain sanctuary—and yet now I am ready to admit that sometimes I felt that we found our forever home too early. I knew I would never leave it and still wondered what it might be like to live elsewhere. More than fantasies of wanderlust, it was like marrying a first love and loving deeply but realizing there was more to experience out there. Now that house is gone. Will we build again? We still don't know. But maybe now we can choose without the woundedness, need, and craving in our way. Maybe I don't need to be rooted as I once thought I did. Maybe this is freedom. Maybe I am now fluid and can bring this strength into all aspects of my life.

Gentle Knock:

What does home mean to you?

Where have you lost the sense of home? Describe the loss.

Where are the places where you have felt most at home? How did factors of people and atmosphere contribute to that feeling?

What about the places that tempted you to make your home? What elements are seductive, comforting, appealing, exciting to different parts of your being?

Some people will spend eternity moving around to avoid being with themselves.

Ultimately, no house or hill or 'hood will save us. At some point we have to stop running away and learn to enjoy our own company. No matter where we go, we take *us* along. On the other hand, we can create a sense of home anywhere, and some places will always remain special.

My mountain sanctuary will always hold a special place in my heart. Miraculously, after rain, grass began to grow on our land, bringing some color and life to the moonscape. Maybe one day we will live there again. Like us, the land is scorched, edgy, raw, tired, and wounded, and yet the will to transform is evident. The dark sooty ground, mangled trees and scorched rocks normalize the pain we still carry. The delicate clumps of green grass remind us of the regenerative power of nature.

The world moves on, yet we will heal gradually with the land. We don't have to rush our process. It will take decades for the land to truly heal. When the world seems to forget our pain, we will be comforted to know the land hasn't forgotten. Eventually, our scars will mend and something new will arise. We can't know yet what it will look like. We can't know yet who we will be. We will discover who we will become together. Every season we will morph and change, yet our hard-earned raw beauty will remain, always a reminder of the power of fire to transform.

Turns out, home is where the heart is. Home is what we say it is. And it is OK to mourn the loss of a home.

Chapter 13:

Waiting 'til I Feel Like It

I've been absolutely terrified every moment of my life—and I've never let it keep me from doing a single thing I wanted to do.

— GEORGIA O'KEEFE

Given the life I have created, I am frequently faced with the opportunity to go out in the world carrying my desire to make a difference by speaking or leading a seminar. And most of the time I don't want to go. I resist. I wonder if I am up to the task. Everything seems to be holding me back, and I find a million other things to do. Even cleaning the cat box seems compelling. I crave the comfort of staying in my pajamas, knowing this would be a much easier, safer, and more comfortable way to live my life.

Yet this is the life I have chosen. Am I crazy? Or is this typical for so many of us who have big dreams and aspirations that take us beyond where we ever thought we would go?

Our human desire for security and safety is sneaky; it makes us want to do nothing other than be comfortable. If we buy into that, we may never be the person we aspire to be, do the things that express our passions, or have the life we desire. If we only dwell in our comfort, the world will probably pass us by, and nothing will change. We may never become who we truly want and are intended to be.

More than ever before, due to my most recent life transition, I now understand what John Lennon meant when he uttered the words, "Life is what happens to you while you're busy making other plans." Life happens, loss happens, illness happens—and houses burn down. People we love die, and ultimately, (of course) we all die. When loss, illness, or tragedy strike, it is easy to ask "why?" But after the dust settles and the initial shock wears off, the transformed among us will ask soul-provoking questions such as: "Who are we going to *be* in the midst of it all? How will we act? What will we do? And will we continue on, even when we don't *feel* like it?"

If your first response to the questions posed above is resistance or even a sense of being overwhelmed, don't be dismayed. Most of us, or at least those of us who are willing to speak the truth, would concur. I, it seems, was born with the first response of "I can't—and besides that, I don't even wanna!" My "I don't wanna" is old and familiar. It's understandable, too. After moving back and forth between my parents' homes, adjusting to new schools and new surroundings—and struggling each time—change brought to my system an inherent resistance. My already tender psyche might have resisted anything new, but after a few public humiliations, I became convinced no good could come of putting myself out there in any way, shape, or form!

I've already told you about my "Chick-a-go moment," as I now fondly refer to it. Everyone has these defining moments. Most of them, we remember. What we don't realize is how much these moments still hold us back in our present life.

One of the key reasons people wait is all this excess baggage we carry with us. It weighs us down and cripples our ability to see life as it is now. Often, the key is the simple realization that we do this and will continue to do this. Then we can catch ourselves in the act and gently return to whatever it is that stands in our way. "Stop, catch, and roll on" is my new motto. Even now, faced with a classroom full of my peers, my hand is full of lead weight if a teacher poses a question. Even now, I get nervous every time I take to the stage.

Gentle Knock:

We all have our methods of procrastination and avoidance when it comes to living our dreams. Stop for a moment and think about your own favorite methods. My mom told me how she spent days ironing Christmas ribbons (in July) to avoid working on her thesis. My friend Tally avoided studying for her bar exam by buying teddy bears online (an obsession that only began when she sat down on her first day to study…). My friend Ellen loses herself in reading when she feels overwhelmed, which she admits is "sneaky," as it seems she is doing something worthwhile.

You might be shocked by just how predictable and repetitive these are. Or you may be amazed at your ingenuity in creating narratives and situations that look so fresh and original…but in reality mask the same familiar fears. Write down some of your patterns.

After surfing some of the ups and downs of life, our desire for safety is even stronger. We may find ourselves shutting down our dreams simply from lack of energy or the seeming inability to put ourselves out there when we are already feeling so taxed. A few months after the fire, I had the opportunity to jump into something that absolutely terrified me. A dear friend of mine spent seventeen years on the road as a professional comedian, and then developed her very own one woman show. Turns out, not long after the fire, she was offering a workshop in stand-up comedy. Never called to be a comedian, but usually called to take a leap, I signed up.

What is funny about losing everything to fire, you might ask? Not much, I would respond. Yet one thing I have counted on is my ability to find humor amidst the darkness. In a quick moment, I said yes to the workshop and in the next moment, I wondered if I had truly lost my mind.

I know, I know, I know, I told my Inner Leaper. Really: Do I need to put my fragile psyche through this? Is this the right time? Will I be perceived as insensitive for making jokes about my experience with the fire?

Regardless of my screaming concerns, I recognized an opportunity and a personal edge. Seeing Kristina perform a multitude of times and admiring her genius, I knew I could learn a lot. My desire came from the challenge and the extreme level of comfort Kristina consistently displayed on stage.

I haven't seen too many people as "at home" in front of a crowd as she. Given that so much of my career involves public speaking, I craved the ease she wore so effortlessly.

During the course, I vacillated between seeing the brilliance in my material and wanting to run for the hills. Kristina stressed memorization, which has never been my strong suit. When I speak, I have an outline. Typically, I know how I will begin and end, but fill in most of the content from what occurs in the moment. Add attempting to be funny on top of this, and it seemed a recipe for disaster—or for me to go as stiff as a board and be oh-so-far from funny. Humiliation, it seemed, lurked right around the corner.

Just so you know, I always sweat before speaking. Even after years of sharing my story in the rooms of Twelve-Step recovery, an invitation to speak in a new venue always brings up anxiety. During my first "real" gig in front of the general public, I had the chance to share the stage with many legends in the field of personal development. Of course, I said "yes," which was followed immediately by several months of ongoing anguish as the event approached. Finally, after many sleepless nights, I had a coaching session with a speaker superstar who gave me a basic formula and helped me craft a beginning, the body, and an ending. Now, with a simple framework from which to hang my material, I had some peace. Though, truth be told, I doubted my ability up until the very moment I took the stage.

I figured that it would get better, that the more I spoke the less I would fear. But it seemed that any offer to speak at the next level of prestige brought waves of anxiety with it.

Before the fire, another big opportunity came my way, and the month prior was one of the biggest roller coaster rides of my life. The angst extreme, I picked up my tool kit and threw myself into my work. I spent time alone, soul-searching, sitting on my glorious deck, gazing at the view, and questioning the meaning of life. Again, I wondered why I might choose to take actions that riled my soul and challenged me to the core. And again, I knew the answer almost as soon as I asked the question—I chose this growing and emerging because it's my path—and I have learned to become willing to walk through the pain and not question where it might lead.

For my comic debut, I slept better than my typical few scattered hours before a big event. Discovering I was to take the stage first brought another level of angst—and also some relief. I wouldn't have to sit in the audience anticipating my time. I could get it over with, then rejoin the crowd and *actually* be present. Finally, the show began. Kristina warmed the crowd with her brilliance and set them up beautifully to receive us with even more love in their hearts than they had already.

My moment came... I fumbled with the microphone and

was blinded by the lights, which truly kept me from making out any faces in the crowd. And I began. Laughs came quickly and easily, surprising me utterly. My mind felt jumbled until a few lines in, and then all of a sudden I was there, present—and alive. A particularly loud gremlin kept telling me to worry that they might not continue laughing as boisterously. I kept going anyway, slowing it down, remembering to wait as people laughed, recalling that pauses are actually funny in themselves and can create a new level of laughter as the joke settles in. As Kristina coached us, it's not so much what we are saying, it's how we are being. And, slowing it down and bringing expression makes the words shine. She also insisted we remain vulnerable—and shared how on the comic stage you can do anything, be anything.

At one point, they cheered so loudly that I thought I should just end right there on the spot. Not wanting to leave the stage, and still having a few more tales, I continued on. It was over in a flash, and I wanted to ride the ride again! One by one, the rest of the group took the stage. Everyone was brilliant, gorgeous, and hilarious. Absolutely none of us had ever done it before—and at least one of us had never been on stage before, ever. Each woman shared real-life stories with perspective and glorious wit, admitting challenges and vulnerabilities with grace. We were all unique yet connected by our spirit of leaping into the unknown. The crowd loved it and cheered us on for the entire show. We all returned to the stage for a final bow and to pat each other on the back. We each knew what it took, what we had to deal with and overcome to be there that night. It took courage!

How many times have we heard that courage isn't the absence of fear? Courage is instead the ability to feel the fear and take action anyway. We hear this and say, "Yeah, I know, I know, just do it and all that." But once the fear takes hold, our first response is a strong desire to run or freeze and hunker down in the tall grass hoping no one sees us. Many people wait to take action until the fear goes away, or they use the sensation of fear as a reason not to do something. So often I hear my clients say, "It (whatever *it* is) is causing me too much anxiety so I decided not to continue." They wait to feel like doing it, and somehow that feeling never comes.

What if the anxiety we feel around taking on new ventures and adventures was just part of the deal? What if it was pretty much ALWAYS part of the deal? What if we really knew this? To grow and stretch ourselves isn't always comfortable and certainly isn't easy. That's why there is a term for it: "growing pains."

Although we don't like to admit it, many of us back off from our goals at the first sign of discomfort. Or we get through the first phase of discomfort and think, "Okay, that's it. I don't have to go through *that* again." And when the next level of "growing pains" occurs, we stop. We think, "I've already gone through this, I'm not doing it again." Or even worse, we think, "Maybe this is a *sign* that I shouldn't be doing this."

Gentle Knock:

When fear arises, the question to ask is: Are you letting it stop you from creating what you want in life or are you going in a direction that no longer aligns with your purpose? Where do you need some courage in your life? Remember, there is nothing wrong with deciding halfway through that you are not on the right path and choosing a new direction.

How do we reconcile these parts of ourselves that are in screaming contradiction to each other? The terrified child is still alive and well and probably always will be. The "I don't wanna, I can't, I won't, no way, no how" part lets me know that not much is a good idea. And, still the part that says "yes" just keeps saying "yes" even though the wail of "nooooooooooo" is hard to miss. If you are able to leave your screaming banshees in the dust, then I am happy for you. Apparently, that is not to be my path in life. My banshees go with me. They are the proverbial insects with a microphone when I really examine them. A lot of bluster with not a lot of substance. In reality I am actually quite safe from their antics, as nothing they predict can actually kill me, but as we know, this just doesn't matter a whole lot at certain moments.

These are the moments where they cloud all vision, all listening, and we can't see or hear anything. What I have learned to do is what I call "point and drive." Just get in the car, head it in the direction I need to go, and drive. Point and drive is sometimes as good as it gets. Another strategy I use to free myself from the fear that attempts to run the show is to name the fear and share it with my trusted advisors. I have people with whom I can share the real, raw deal. Like: "Arrrrrrrrrgh," which actually translates to: "My terror wants to take me out. Help!" During the writing of my first book, there were countless times I considered giving up. Having never written a book before, often it really didn't seem like a good idea. Yet write, I did. And, slowly but surely, a book took form. There were countless nights of lost sleep and days of anxiety and doubt, but, one word at time, I continued my journey.

If you are a self-doubter like I am, find the people who love you, who can listen to you and your fears, hearing it all—and not believing a word of it. Find the friends who won't try to fix you but instead will offer love, hugs, and deep, penetrating looks into your soul, and in their eyes you will see the truth that in fact you can do what you fear you can't.

Remember, your "I don't wanna" will pass. If you are following your heart, and are merely stopped by fear, it will pass on by. This is an excellent time to practice waiting! You can wait longer than the fear that grips you. Wait for it to ease, wait for it to shift, wait for it to go. Moods are funny. They seem to be the truth in a moment of passion or despair. Mostly, I have learned not to trust my moods to determine my actions. If I did, truly, I would not do anything. At all. Nothing. Nada. I especially wouldn't be a writer!

I have definitely found my home among the other twisted artist-types who aren't afraid to share their darkness about life and the craft itself. These musings are plentiful and help remind me I haven't quite gone over the edge. Thanks to Gene Fowler, I know that "Writing is easy: All you do is sit staring at a blank sheet of paper until drops of blood form on your forehead." Ray Bradbury reminds me "You must stay drunk on writing so reality cannot destroy you." Anne Lamott's entire book *Bird by Bird* could keep me sane, or at least normalize my insanity. She speaks the truth when she says, "You can get the monkey off your back, but the circus never leaves town," in her book *Grace (Eventually): Thoughts on Faith.*

These fine folks remind me I am not alone. They grant me the permission to write my truth, even if it's not the entire truth. Really, I know there is sunshine up there, even when the clouds roll in. And, good God, I am still in the grief process. So, being here, I can't help baring it all. If it touches one heart, opens up one mind, gives one iota of freedom to a fellow traveler, that's good enough for me. I am in the trenches of life, marveling at the muck and grime, while still having moments of grace and beauty when it all clicks, before falling apart once again. Yesterday I laughed uproariously, today I cry like a baby.

There *are* times to jump into life. And, there are times to pause and reflect. With patience and practice, we can learn to distinguish between the two. So many of our fears are those garden-variety ones such as lack of worth. Jumping in these moments feels invigorating and inspires a new level of performance.

At a lecture given by Jack Canfield (author of *Chicken Soup for the Soul*), I was presented with a split-second decision about whether to jump into action or stay glued to my chair. Partway through his talk, Jack held up a hundred-dollar bill and asked, "Who wants this?" As I scrambled from my chair and ran for the stage, I chose to listen to my desire versus my screaming voices telling me I was making a dreadful mistake. Of course, that was also the point of his exercise. But until he said, "Yes, that's it!" I wasn't sure. In those moments of being in the unknown, when the game hasn't been played out and we don't quite know how it will go, it's easy to quit. Instead, that action propelled me forward and became a metaphor for how I lived my life. The lesson: Don't over-think it, don't stop, and don't wait. Jump into the unknown and see. Say yes!

The freedom I felt from my willingness to jump and risk without knowing for sure if it was the right thing to do was exhilarating. Jumping in that moment led to more and more movement out of my comfort zone into a new world of which I had only previously dreamed. My action that day propelled me forward into becoming a first-time author and a speaker, launching my radio show, and many other fabulous things. The flip side was that sometimes I thought I needed to jump at times when my system cried "NO!" During these moments, I was thrown into a quandary and wondered: "Was I failing myself if I didn't jump? Was I chickening out? Was I losing my edge or my game? Was I missing out?"

We all have our natural inclination. If you tend to pause

and over-think, it may be time to jump. If you tend to jump into everything, it may be time to practice waiting.

There are clearly times when to jump is the best thing. Then there are times when patience pays. There are times when we just don't know what is right or what we should do. Maybe that time between is an opportunity to expand. Maybe we need to sit some jumps out, and other times jump fast when our butts are glued to the chair. Maybe sometimes we need to do something else entirely.

Gentle Knock:

Do you know when it's time to jump and when it's time to stay put? How can you tell if you are being patient or if you are chickening out? Can you allow yourself those times to let the dust settle to gain clarity on what you really want?

In the months since the fire, I have had the unique opportunity to be in two places at once. On one hand, I am in the midst of writing this book and working on deadlines, engaging both hemispheres of my brain—the logical and the creative. On the other hand, I am letting my grief be what it is, letting myself ride that ride and feel what there is to feel, while still not knowing where it might take me.

What do we do when we are moving toward one of our life goals and suddenly the fear shows up, and the inspiration vanishes into thin air? I have found that underappreciated old-fashioned word "commitment" to be my greatest ally in times of questioning, struggle, and plain old self-doubt. I have also found it to be the greatest weapon against my "I don't wanna" when in fact I really do wanna. For instance, writing this book is something I really want.

Let's explore "commitment" for a moment. Typically, we romanticize our dreams, and typically aren't big fans of commitment. Yet without a true commitment, what begins as a dream merely stays in the ether and is never realized.

So what are we to do? First we must make a commitment, then we must put our butts on the line and honor that commitment. Commitment trumps all excuses. It doesn't matter if you don't "feel" like staying married today if you are committed. Yes, we need the initial inspiration. The passion is helpful. The vision is mighty. Your "burning why" is essential. A healthy support system is wonderful. All these things are important contributing factors, but when the chips are down, the mood is low, the wind is cold, the coffee is gone, the running shoes are muddy, the knee is blown out, the house burns down—all that is left is our commitment.

To honor our commitments, we must walk through our own fire. It isn't easy. It's often scary. Long-distance runners (like my sister-in-law) come home with blisters and missing toenails. And they still do it! I can't claim to have any blisters on my typing fingers, although sometimes my wrists ache. I can tell you that it often feels painful. I am afraid. I am concerned. I am daunted, to say the least. I have thrown my hat over the fence and said yes to my new publisher. I have committed to this endeavor. I will honor that commitment—and again, I will know myself as greater than I feel in this moment. That's what really matters. It's not so much what we produce, it's how we experience ourselves after (and during) our honoring of a commitment we've made to ourselves.

It's helpful to make the commitment to others, as most of us get sloppy simply making commitments to ourselves. We let ourselves off the hook way too early and way too fast, and then we don't trust what comes out of our mouths. We then begin to believe the lie that we couldn't do it anyway—or worse yet, we sell out on our dream. So making the commitment to someone else who will actually hold us to that commitment is the way to go.

Do you want to know what happens when I sit down to write and face the blank screen, fingers on the keyboard? Screaming monkeys. Bullying banshees. Argumentative gargoyles. All telling me their lies, which sound like: *I can't do it, I won't do it, and I don't even want to do it.* That is the human (my human, and I would argue yours too) mechanism at work. That is why I wait. That is why *we* wait.

But I return to it because I am clear. This is what I want to be doing. This is what I choose to be doing. This is my passion. And this is my commitment.

Gentle Knock:

Take some time to review your commitments. Why do you have them? Are you honoring your word? Are you letting yourself off the hook? Are you willing to do what it takes to stay true to your path, if you know you are living your purpose? Where is your "I don't wanna" giving you a healing message? Where are you not listening? When you make a commitment that turns out to be wrong for you—that is, you know it in your bones you are not in the right place or with the right person for the right reasons—do you know how to acknowledge your mistake and create a new commitment?

Just as I am clear about honoring my commitment to writing this book and not being bought off by my "I don't wanna's," I am equally clear in my allowance of my grieving process and my lack of interest in forcing myself to be somewhere other than where I am. Our culture wants to hurry through grief and wrap it up in a neat package. We have the tools; we have the technology, so we think we should be somewhere other than where we are. We have a "quick fix" society. Slap a bandage on it and jump back in the game.

Would we scream at the fire-ravaged land and say, "Hurry up and heal"? Well maybe, in our sorrow. But would we truly expect that? My land is scorched, the trees blackened, the earth parched. You can't walk across it without getting covered in ash and soot. Can I tell it to clean itself up NOW?

Instead, I will take my time. I choose to see the beauty in the world—and I choose to experience the horror. I choose to allow my dogs' love to fill me up—and I allow my loss to empty me out. I choose all of this for as long as I need to.

I am evolving and will not emerge a moment too soon.

Chapter 14:

Waiting for the Other Shoe to Drop

Thar she blows!
— OLD WHALING QUOTE, UTTERED BY
MY HUSBAND WHEN I BLOW MY LID

On initial viewing, my husband and I may seem OK, but if you come closer and peer into our souls you may see the burning embers of our sadness. Push us a little too far in either direction, and sometimes things blow apart. Yesterday, a silly fight with my husband over our cat, my tired mind, a looming writing deadline—they all came together in a perfect storm which took me out of "normal" into excessive trigger-ability. And, yes, my first response is still to run screaming for the hills. This time, I didn't run, and we are friends again.

After the fire, I hoped David and I would never fight again, that our loss would bond us more deeply than that. It has, of course, bonded us deeply. And I still have my fears. I still have my moments. I am still a messy human. And of course, we still occasionally fight.

In many cases of trauma, the most upsetting part is the surprise. David and I didn't know that this really terrible thing was going to happen—we were caught totally off guard. Now our anxious minds remain vigilant, grinding their teeth, rigidly on the lookout for the NEXT awful thing so at least we won't be so utterly astounded by shameful not-knowing or blissful ignorance. We've been shocked and scared and confused and frightened out of our "normal" state of mind. Our skin is thin, our resistance is low, and our filters are off. We are primarily doing one kind of waiting: for the next terrible thing to happen, waiting for the other shoe to drop.

The shoe dropped in the form of an acquaintance who got very angry with me when I least expected it. She said she needed to get some things off her chest—something I am all in favor of—but I didn't realize what she wanted to say had to do with me. As she began telling me how I had wronged her, my heart thumped in my chest, yet I knew I wasn't up for a fight... Or so I thought.

Instead I bit fast—hook, line, and sinker—and got angry back. And no surprise—it didn't go very well. After we both hung up the phone in anger, I knew I would keep worrying and obsessing about the interaction, so I called her back and attempted to have it go a little better.

It's an amazing experience to hear another's view of us that is so diametrically opposed to our own self-image that we barely recognize this person ourselves. It's disorienting, to say the least. In a moment of blessed clarity, I realized all I could do was apologize.

So what did I do after this interaction? Did my willingness to attempt to make things right propel me into a new realm of spiritual connection and love for all humanity? Not quite... Instead, I fell into a pit of extreme despair. Always companions waiting for the right moment, the gremlins wailed loudly: *The world is not safe, you will be misunderstood, there are people who don't like you or get you, all these people will gather together and bring their evidence. It's happening right now. People are talking about you. They think you are self-centered. They are tired of your grief...* And blah blah blah and more blah.

And what did I do with all these disruptive visitors? I took them to the mall. Writing this, I realize some ancient irony. Many moons ago, during the years of my addiction and disorders, I would binge-shop while I binge-ate, wandering malls aimlessly, feeling the dark pit of despair closing in and numbing myself with food and spending.

Now my demons were with me as I made a few stops at the mall. As I walked into a store where the saleswomen were half my age, I made the split-second decision that my shoes were tacky and absolutely did not go with the dress I was wearing (there's that old shoe thing again). Until this moment, I thought my outfit was A-OK. Flashbacks loomed, of high school and the cheerleaders decreeing my shoes tacky... And, guess what: I couldn't let it go. Could not. Would not. Instead of rallying my tender psyche, I folded and bought some sandals, wearing them out of the store and burying the shoes I had been wearing in a bag. Seriously! The whole time, I was observing myself do this, falling into this age-old trap of waiting to be universally loved and admired.

Here's the breakdown. What happened: Someone I know said I was inconsiderate and she was angry with me. What I made it mean: The world is not safe, I am not safe, and worst of all, my shoes are not right. Again. Even after all these years and all this training, in this particular moment I was no good and my only hope was a different pair of shoes.

Of course, there are plenty of times I am much more lean, mean, and spiritually serene, and don't get triggered so easily. And when I do get triggered, I return to peaceful equilibrium—without the aid of new footwear.

So what are we to do when we just can't pull our heads out of our own messes?

Return to that cultivated sense of deep friendship for a soul-shaking cry. So, this day, I turned to another friend, Dusty. I will elaborate my admiration for that exquisite creature who shines her light so brightly for so many. There are lights in the world, and then there is Dusty: a light so luminous that it doesn't just fill a room, it overwhelms it. Darkness melts in her presence and we lesser-lit folk become whole simply being in her space.

Making myself horribly wrong for my foray into the darkness, I called Dusty, who made it right. Through the phone she patted me on the head and reminded me that first of all, I am OK. Secondly, everything is OK. And, finally, I can let go. Then she said something like, "Jiminy Cricket people (she actually used different words...)! Just whose expectations are we living up to anyway?" She reminded me that I am an emotional creature, have had just a few things going on lately, and if I took a walk on the wild side of my mind—well then, that was OK too.

I breathed in the love and wisdom that poured through the phone line and remembered that the people I want in my life are those who will get messy, feel deeply, express strongly, make mistakes, blow snot, and moan like she-devils. If we can't truly unwind and unravel with our peeps, what the heck is the point?

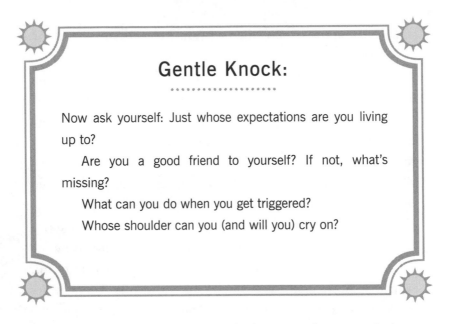

Gentle Knock:

Now ask yourself: Just whose expectations are you living up to?

Are you a good friend to yourself? If not, what's missing?

What can you do when you get triggered?

Whose shoulder can you (and will you) cry on?

We all have our shadow side, whether it surfaces regularly or not. It is there. So many people stuff their shadow down deep, and it sneaks out in other delightful disguises—substance abuse, overeating, overspending, workaholism, sex addiction, domestic violence, or whatever your own personal brand of disguised, dispossessed pain or worry might be.

We read the papers, watch the news, and are bombarded with the horrendous things happening in the world. It's easy to live in fear of the unknown, of what danger might lurk around the next corner. Some of us internalize the horror; allowing it to slowly suck us dry. Some of us have been like this for as long as we can remember. For others, the spark got ignited by some long-ago life event where our world suddenly shifted. A death in the family, divorce of parents, abuse, or simply an awkward moment with our peers. We then go through life protecting our tender hearts from further trauma, wanting the best in the world but continually seeing evidence of the worst.

Stress does bad things to people. Grief affects even the strongest of souls. Trauma can mess us up for a while. Others may not need such a monumental event and simply go through life with a milder, and equally damaging, form of needing to protect.

Alicia, a stay-at-home mom of three gorgeous girls, tells such a tale:

> *The truth is nothing really "terrible" has happened in my life. I had a normal childhood, grew up in the same town where my parents grew up, attended the same school system all my life, went off to college, and married my first love. Even though crazy things happened in the world around me, somehow my family was never touched. And, that's part of the problem. Since I have been seemingly blessed, I now have the irrational belief that my time is coming. Any day now, that is.*

Now, with my three precious girls at school age, my anxiety is greater than ever. I read the headlines, hear the news... and am frightened by this world and all its crazy happenings. I share my fears with my husband, but he has stopped listening and sometimes thinks I am crazy. Not to say he is not without his concerns. He is a good dad, and in my moments of calm I can see that he has a "healthy" balance of concern. He keeps the girls safe, out of harm, but is absolutely sure he doesn't want to live in paranoia. I, on the other hand, do live in paranoia. I stay up late at night Googling any new symptom one of the girls might have. Bloody nose? Ah, must be a brain tumor. Excessive coughing? Let's cut out all allergens, toxins, pollutants, chemicals... We will remove the carpet, the dogs, and the gluten.

Yes, I have started to have some humor in my madness. It's not quite this extreme, but close. It drives me day and night. Yet I know that, no matter what danger I uncover, there is always another one looming. I finally broke down and found a therapist. She is helping me to stay in the moment, loosen my grasp and my false sense of control—and actually spend some time taking care of myself. I still fall into my worrying pattern, but I recognize it and can put a halt to it more quickly. It's like reaching for the cookie jar. Sometimes we have already eaten the cookie before we realize we weren't going to. Sometimes we stop before we put it in our mouths. Sometimes we go and have a carrot instead. And now I celebrate when I catch myself—and am gentler when I don't. I realize I can't wait for life to settle down. I still get scared about what might be around the next corner, but I definitely have more peace about the unpredictable nature of life. And, the bottom line: I know that, no matter what happens, I will be OK.

While I was still moving through my extreme angst and grief over the fire and losing my home, I attended a business seminar. For those first few hours among "normal folks" in the workshop, I felt like a leper. I didn't belong or fit in among these shiny (and clean) classmates. Yes, I had bathed, but the stain of ash still remained on my feet (literally) and in my heart (metaphorically but just as painfully black, or so it felt to me).

I had to get away from these people, these shiny professionals who had most likely just emerged from homes with walk-in closets. So I fled. As it turned out, however, a "playing hooky" break in the California sunshine and far from home was just what I needed. I took the afternoon off, had a delicious meal which led to a stroll by the beach. I wandered all afternoon with perfect weather as my companion. On the way to the airport, I watched the palm trees passing by and wanted to do anything, *anything,* but board that plane back to Colorado. Leaving Los Angeles and returning to a state that was still on fire was almost too much. To what was I returning? Where was I going? Where would I stay? Was anything really safe?

Of course, when I arrived, there was a place to stay and there were some safe things.

I returned to the cozy basement at Jessica's and knew that in the morning I could spend time with her angel girls. Pretending to bite off their noses, serving up their breakfast cereal, letting them feed Tigger, watching them strut around the house in their princess finery. The giggles, the hugs, the love—I soaked it all up. Buzzing energy fields of curiosity as well as tempestuous little goddesses in their own right, Jessica's girls know how to fill up a space with excellent juju.

I let them wash my mind of worry. I let myself be in the moment with them before they left for their day of adventure.

I absorbed their goodness and their spunk and wondered to myself, just how do we live without living in fear? How do we not simply wait for the other shoe to drop? This is the question of our age. We extra-sensitive types need to find outlets and distractions from the angst. My outlet in California was playing hooky from class. Other times, it's a walk with my dogs, a pedicure, a great movie, or a bad TV series.

Gentle Knock:

What do you think about healthy distractions? Which ones work for you?

How does the easy proliferation of twenty-four-hour news affect you? How often do you use your television or the Internet to absorb everything you can about the latest disaster? Do you make a distinction between being informed and being inundated?

Pretend your Highest, Wisest, Oldest Self had some advice to offer me in California or Alicia on Google—what do you think it might say? What would that self have to say about the places you wait because you're worried something even more terrible will happen?

My crazed moments of angst on steroids are blessedly rare, but when they occur I seem to be swallowed whole. This is the existential angst that philosophers have discussed for eons. These moments are like Edward Munch's painting "The Scream," a face twisted in anguish, a body swirling into nothingness. It is the grasping for safety in an unsafe world. It is the desperate seeking of grounded-ness as we float through the universe suspended only by gravity. There is no ground, it does not exist. There is no certainty. There are no guarantees. It's the knowing that, just because something terrible happens, we are not protected from more horrific events. One wise friend admonished, "No one is entitled to a perfect life." She should know. Her two children died as the car driven by a babysitter stalled out on a railroad track. Then a short time later her husband died of cancer.

There are gifts that come from destruction, but they often come wrapped in barbed wire. We don't know they are gifts at the time—and the truth is, they are only gifts if we are willing to see, if we are willing to shift our perspective enough. Some big bad things require a very big shift, an ultimate opening of consciousness that doesn't come easily when we are lying panting, gasping from our wounds on the floor. Many people can't or don't, and they end up bitter to the end, always feeling cheated by the world and its people.

At this point in life, I realize that no matter how wise I might feel at times, I will be thrown again. After I go through one of these occasions and cry on one of my friends' shoulders or even on my own, I feel lighter.

Thank God for my tools. Thank God for my training. Thank God for my ability to stop in the moment and to have some semblance of sanity even in the midst of my insanity. So, each time I choose life and in choosing I am aware that it is *all* just a choice.

Gentle Knock:

In times of great stress or trauma (or just even in prolonged times when we feel blue), sometimes we forget our tools or feel we don't have any at all. In these times, it is important that we know when to say "when" and reach out for help. In addition to my Twelve-Step meetings, the support of friends and loved ones, and my writing, I went back into therapy after the fire to gain even more tools. Other ideas are support groups, physical exercise, a nurturing diet, prayer, and meditation. Sometimes we need more serious intervention, in which case consult with your medical doctor or therapist about what you might need.

As Colorado continued to burn all summer, I crossed off my list of worries my fear of losing my home to a forest fire. Then, for a moment, I wondered: Could our land burn again? Is there enough fuel on the ground? Is the universe that cruel? Is someone up there making these choices for our fate?

But really, most likely it won't happen again; they say lightning doesn't strike in the same place twice. Or it might. But instead of living in concern, I live. Just live.

What am I waiting for? Maybe I am just waiting for the world to make sense. And, yes, if this is so, I realize I may wait a long, long time. But the question remains: What will I do while I'm waiting for that answer?

Chapter 15:

Waiting for God to Show Up

You know what the Lama says to me?
[He says]: "When you die, on your deathbed,
you will receive total consciousness."
So I got that goin' for me, which is nice.

—BILL MURRAY
AS CARL SPACKLER IN *CADDYSHACK*

With a white-knuckle grip on the steering wheel and the speedometer pegged at exactly eight miles over the limit, the mantra coming from my lips was, "I am going to miss my plane. I am going to miss my plane. I just know it." Now, since we're all fully immersed practitioners in the land of self-help, we know that such self-talk is simply negative creation, absolutely not the right way to practice the good law of attraction, and certainly devoid of any empowering context!

The self-defeating message running below this commentary ("I am such a f-up, I am such a f-up") really put the cherry on the cake. I pondered all of this as I donned my flip-flops to run from security to my gate. *Does the universe appreciate that I am running? Would the universe frown if I stopped to catch my breath? Does the universe actually care? Is there really a Being to whom I can pray to make my flight? Really? Is that how God works? Does he really have time for that?*

As I pondered the sad news headlines I read that morning, I questioned further. Will God answer my prayer and hold my flight so I don't compromise my precious trip to California, and somewhere else a child slips into a lake and drowns? Did that child not pray hard enough? Were the parents attracting some age-old karma? Did they forget to say please or thank you? Really?

I made my flight. I did give thanks to something, maybe to the "god of trivial events" or the "god of aeronautics" or maybe just to God whoever he, she, it, or they may be. Even our available pronouns reveal how obscure and mysterious this source of Good may be. How are we supposed to communicate with something our language has no ability to contain or define?

After my house burned down, I faced what one might call a spiritual crisis. Always a believer in *some* power greater than myself, I allowed myself to question everything. Perhaps most importantly, "Is there something or someone that cares about me, and if so, why would that something destroy my most beloved and cherished sanctuary? What did I do or not do that earned that result? Or, if it had nothing to do with me, and such events are completely random, and if anything can happen to anyone at any time, what is the point of this whole thing?"

Albert Einstein said the most important question we can ask ourselves is whether or not we live in a universe that is friendly to our desires and purpose. He argued that you can divide people into three categories: those who believe in a Force that is unfriendly to human desires, those who believe in a perfectly neutral playing field, and those who believe there is something Good and It is inherently on our side, as we are on Its side.

As I toss all my beliefs on the ground, I stomp on them until they lie bleeding—and then start picking them back up with a fresh look to see what works and what fits now. I haven't picked up all the pieces. I am still seeing just how they fit—and sometimes I leave them squirming helplessly on the ground as they beg for my attention, consideration, and final verdict. I may leave them in the mud and ash or simply walk away. They may cry out as I turn my back. And sometimes I escape it all by watching some mind-numbing TV movie of the week. We sober people have very few ways to really tune out...

Recently, I heard someone say that any crisis after the age of forty is a spiritual crisis, and since I am on the backside of my mid-forties, I choose to buy into this idea. Ultimately, we need to work out on our own what any crisis means. We can be influenced by teachings, literature, religion, art, or wise men and women, yet it's still crucial we each find our own way. My mentor offered a mantra I have been repeating since she first passed it on to me—*walk your own path.* Walk my own path. My own. Not yours, not how you think I should be or how you think you should be or how religion or any spiritual teaching thinks we should be. Not the teachings of a particular school, education, or group. Your own. My own.

Eckhart Tolle also recommends we turn aside from all theory and consult our own experience—what actually happens when we set aside (even for a brief moment) all our stories and judgments and experience firsthand the joy that vibrates in the Now. Which is probably the reason that *The Power of Now* is the best-selling spiritual book of the past fifty years. When Tolle is asked a question, instead of answering, he encourages us to step outside our mind and see what's occurring right now in our experience. This is especially mind-bending if you're just reading about it, and when you actually do it, it makes the world absolutely shift on its axis.

I choose to see my recent crisis as an opportunity to truly walk my own path. I have been exploring what that means for many years, yet I still wanted to do it "right." As Bill, my beloved mentor says, "You can get to the top of a mountain on a donkey named Bob." I heard those words, but being the rule follower and good girl I am (or was), I craved to find the "proper" channel instead of giving myself the freedom to find my own way. Many of us want to do things right, especially in the area of religion or spirituality. And, if we have spent any time around religion, it definitely seems there are right ways and wrong ways. What is an enlightened seeker to do?

It's quite powerful when we see the difference between knowing "you must find your own path" because that's what wise people say, and knowing your own path because you found it and it is sweet. Or the difference between knowing "God" exists because some people say so and it seems like a nice idea that takes away some of the pain and annoyance and unfairness of life (which is a perfectly good kind of knowing), and knowing God or Good exists because you experience it for yourself.

Gentle Knock:

What does walking your own path mean to you? What gifts have come from loss or crisis in your own life? Could you see the gifts at the time? If not, how were you able to see them? If you haven't seen any good that has come, are you willing to look again?

As I continue my recent spiritual reinvention, in a recent Twelve-Step meeting I heard a slogan that I have heard for many years: "There but for the grace of God go I." It's a lovely sentiment, yet when removed from the context of the literature it takes on a life of its own. Some who utter this slogan seem to be saying that those of us who have survived alcoholism have been chosen. Even more now, I absolutely refuse to believe that anyone is chosen over another. I believe we can choose to tap into God's grace and bring it into our lives, but the idea that there is a God up there picking some and not others is preposterous. How would God choose exactly? "Okay, burn down that one's house, not that one. Keep this one sober, not that other scruffier-looking one. Oh maybe her too 'cause she certainly will do good things. That one? Fugget about it!"

And what about the people who don't choose to tap into God's grace? Would it still be present anyway, and they just wouldn't notice it or identify it in such a way? Or would they be extra screwed?

More than twenty-three years ago, I was given the choice of recovery. At a crossroads in life, I saw darkness looming in my future. Actually, darkness is an inadequate word; it was a huge, black, nasty hole coming to swallow me up. I chose the unknown—with the aid of my parents—and entered rehab. I don't believe God selected me but didn't select my ex-boyfriend, Larry, who died in 2003 of an overdose. God didn't choose me over the poor souls who perished in our fire. Life just happens. Shit just happens. Bad shit just happens. And good shit, too. Yes, it is relative what we label "good shit" and "bad shit." Once upon a time, I would have argued a stronger case for "nothing means anything but the meaning we give it..." But try arguing the case of "it's all up to interpretation" to those raped and pillaged in war, or to the loved ones of a victim of a drunk driver, or to those who lost their parents or wife in a fast-moving fire. Go ahead and make that argument and see what comes back. I'll wait. For some strange reason people don't like it when you suggest their tragedies are ontologically meaningless and could "mean" just about anything!

Truly believing (and having experienced) Freud's words, *"One day in retrospect the years of struggle will strike you as the most beautiful,"* I knew that on the other side of my current life-altering event would be beauty, growth, and hard-earned wisdom. I choose this view. And again, it's up to each of us to find our own meaning that works.

It's true that many people who survive a crisis express gratitude for that crisis *later on*, having come to see meaning and beauty in retrospect. Sometimes the event itself still seems horrific but who we become as a result is the gift. As I've seen over and over in the rooms of recovery, what once seemed like the worst hell of all led to a life beyond imagination. Over and over, people turn from the gates of insanity, imprisonment, or death and choose a life of sobriety. It is truly miraculous to witness, and to experience it is mind-blowing.

There are certain events—such as losing a loved one, receiving a life-altering diagnosis, surviving a devastating forest fire—that really encourage us to ponder the Infinite. Am I waiting to have a relationship with God, or am I deconstructing the one I had, as many do in the face of a crisis? Is this my way of cultivating an even deeper relationship with the Divine? Does God hate me? Am I cursed by karma? Did I not have enough character already? Do we live in a meaningless and random universe? Each of us has to find our own truth. Really, what's the point of our trip around this rock if we don't get to discover for ourselves what life is all about? And we may be wrong. No one actually knows. Through spirituality, we attempt to make sense of the nonsensical. You say you worship fairies? Then worship fairies. You love Jesus? Have Jesus. You see truth in the Old Testament? More power to you. You think nothing is real? Choose that. Choose what works for you. For now, I am letting myself not know what my beliefs will be.

But then I saw one of the most intense rainbows I have ever seen, the colors sharp against the graying sky. I pulled over to take a picture and couldn't find my phone anywhere. I searched to no avail until the rainbow faded a bit. It continued to shimmer in front of me as I made my way up the mountain. Wondering if the pot of gold pointed to my burned property, I considered many views of this encounter. What does it mean? Is this God speaking to me? Are my angels singing their songs? Ultimately, I decided that it was light reflecting on moisture—no more and no less. But that didn't make it any less glorious.

It turns out that the pot of gold didn't end at my property. But our Airstream trailer's sleek silver profile was there to greet me, as was the tail end of one of those revered Rocky Mountain sunsets.

Roberta, a sassy woman in her mid-fifties, shared a story that made me stop and consider things even more deeply:

Before I got sober, I was brash and cocky and absolutely hated God. My parents were killed in a car accident when I was ten, and after that I was shuttled between various households until I went off to college. College was a disaster, I drowned my grief in booze and drugs, played hard, hung with a shady crowd, and bottomed out early. After my third DUI, I spent some time behind bars. A local Twelve-Step group brought a recovery meeting to the jail each week. I was required to go, and I did so with all the venom I could muster. There was too much talk about "God" and even when they said "Higher Power" I wanted to gag.

One day, it rained so hard we couldn't go outside at all. Thunder and lightning crashed, gallons of rain poured in through cracks in the windows—it was a deluge. The next day, I got my needed breath of fresh air (and smoke break) and, as I dropped my cigarette butt to the ground and went to smash it with my foot, I saw something in the brightest purple I have ever seen. Kneeling down to get a closer look, I saw that a tiny flower had pushed its way up through a crack in the cement. I quickly glanced around the rest of the fenced-in yard and all I saw was dusty gravel as far as the eye could see. Nothing living had ever grown in this rugged pen before, of that I was sure.

As I stared at this delicate flower, something happened that I can't quite explain. It was like the shades fell from my eyes, the scales shed from my skin. I felt an aliveness I hadn't experienced since before my parents died. I remembered a day we spent together at the park. My parents so in love, my dad teasing my mom and carrying me around on his shoulders. Suddenly, it was like a camera zooming in to my mom's face. Shocked, I saw what was tucked behind her ear, a gift from my dad. It was a purple flower, the same color as the flower I had just seen. I broke down in sobs, filled with heartbreaking love for my parents, but also, at the same time, a space of peace and acceptance for myself. In that moment, I realized there was something bigger than me out there in the universe, or perhaps in all of us. Something changed on that day that has never changed back. I am not saying I am forever without doubts or even know what to call what I felt. Yet I am no longer angry with "God"—and I found peace within myself.

For so long, I wanted God to show up in an obvious form and prove he was real. I might have heard Roberta's story and bellowed, "Where's my purple flower?!" as the rainbows surrounded me. In other words, there have been many times I miss the miracle that is right in front of me.

Today, as I scramble out the door for a day in town, I know I will surely forget something—it is inevitable. But I won't forget, at least for today, to look for the rainbows out there in the world. I will talk to my clients from my mobile office, write on the fly, swear at the slow drivers, and then mouth, "I'm sorry." I will wonder about the future, and I will do my best to focus being in today. I will shed a tear or more with David as we celebrate one more task accomplished from our enormous post-fire to-do list. Which for some reason seems to keep getting bigger instead of smaller.

I am finally learning to trust myself—to trust my mistakes, chaos, forgetfulness, nastiness, laughter, joy, wisdom, strength, tears, love, and more. There is something I can count on. I am not sure of what it is, exactly. I don't know what to call it yet. Maybe it's God. Maybe it's gravity. Maybe it's the knowledge that this too shall pass. Maybe it's the wisdom that comes with age.

Maybe it's Rumi's sage words: *There is a morning inside you waiting to burst open into Light.*

Gentle Knock:

How are you waiting to deepen your own relationship with the Divine? Do you wait for God to reveal him or herself? Do you look for the Divine in the day-to-day of your life?

Do you feel cared for by Something Greater, that the Divine takes an interest in your prayers, preferences, and activities? If so, which things are OK to ask about and which things still feel "off limits" somehow?

How has your relationship to a Higher Power changed over the years? How has your understanding and experience of this relationship affected your feelings about safety and risk?

Chapter 16:

Knowing When to Say When

I used to be different, now I am the same.
—WERNER ERHARD,
FOUNDER OF EST

In the flash of an eye, my gargantuan self-help library turned to ash. Strangely enough, much of my driven nature has burned away with those books that tried to teach me to be better, stronger, faster, and at the same time more peaceful, whole, and complete. Along with the books were binders full of notes from my graduate school studies, massage training, and personal growth workshops. Journals and vision boards vaporized along with CDs and workbooks offering wisdom to entrepreneurs in the form of list building, business management, and more. It's all gone now.

Many books and binders remained unopened, unread, and unimplemented with their "to-dos" blaring from my shelves. "You are not doing enough," I frequently heard them call. "You need to, you should, you have to, you must. Hurry up, don't forget, don't miss out. Don't mess it up. You are missing opportunities. Now is the time. Hurry hurry hurry." I hear their ghosts still singing to me. No, I say. I won't listen any longer. I won't fall into the trap I once did.

If you think I am cynical about self-help, I am not. Well, maybe not completely. The truth is, self-help doesn't trap us. We trap us. As I dare write a book that will be classified as "self-help," I continue to unearth this dilemma. Self-help has fed me, paid my bills, and given me tools I never had before. I will attempt to walk the fine line between enjoying this beautiful and worthy path and being engulfed by the fire of its often artificial urgency.

The problem is that many of us are actually addicted to self-improvement. When I had this shocking realization for myself, the answer wasn't to take one more course in how to manage my addiction to self-help, it was to peer behind the curtain at what was really going on. Some of us get stuck on a "self-help treadmill." We are determined to find answers but on a deep level, a level often kept hidden away from our awareness, we remain unsatisfied. We end up starving in the midst of plenty.

Gentle Knock:

Do you crave to be different? Do you spend large amounts of time wishing you could change? Do you hope that just maybe, if you did change, life would be better?

When you are presented with new chances to learn and grow, do you have trouble distinguishing between authentically great new information/methodologies and yet another "Get Rich/Perfect/One-with-God Quick" message?

Do you feel that there is still a SECRET secret secret that you don't know and that life will be "better" once you discover it?

For the moment (and this could always change!) check in with your current relationship to "self-help" or "transformation." Does "self-help" bring you increasing joy and freedom, or increasing pressure to be different than you are? Or both?

Many of us go through life striving for just that. We take the next workshop, read the next book, follow the next guru all with a burning desire to become someone new. Then the dust settles, the newness wears off, and we wake up and stare in the mirror, and whom do we see? The same person we saw before. This can be a great disappointment. At least, it always was for me. After each stride in personal growth, I hoped to be different. After a weekend training in Shamanism, I hoped to be different. After giving a talk in a new venue that challenges my fears, I hoped to be different. After writing my first book, I hoped to be different. I could say that this might be the most prevailing and persistent story of my life, perhaps a good epitaph for my gravestone: "I hoped to be different and I was a little bit but not really noticeably so."

I often wondered:

When did self-help become synonymous with "there's something wrong with me"? Or with anyone?

How did it become about the eternal search for something, a search outside the self?

Why did it become about needing the perfect teacher, book, course, or practice?

How did it become about something out there on the horizon?

When did it become a dirty word?

It's time to take this down to the bare bones. Just what is

really going on here? How can so many of us go through life so profoundly dissatisfied?

The common theme is that we never quite settle in. We keep going and going, peeling back more and more layers of the proverbial onion, hoping one day we will find the truth about life and ourselves. One fine day (always in the future), we will arrive and everything will make sense. We will finally be OK. We will be "fixed."

After the fire (for the first time in a very long time), I wasn't inclined to read self-help books. Occasionally someone would suggest a book on grief, but I found that most (if not all) of them talked about grief due to death or illness. Always looking for ways to undermine my process, I felt these books merely suggested that I was lucky not to have *that* kind of loss going on. I also didn't crave anything that promised the "Five Easy Steps to Move through Grief with Joy and Ease" or some such nonsense.

Instead, I talked, I wept, I wrote—and occasionally I read books, but only from those authors who weren't afraid to show their soft underbellies.

Then a new book grabbed my attention. Drawn to the title, I thought, "Ah, *this* author is a kindred soul." Reading her story, I related, connected, and felt she was describing me. But then I read on. And on. Instead of an original tale of a specific human being to which I continued to relate, the narrative degenerated (or so it seemed to me) into the typical tried-and-true self-help formula. Here is that formula, just in case you're not familiar with it:

I was like this: angry/addicted/fat/alone/broke... (Fill in the blank)

Then this happened, and...I was transformed!

After that point, my life has never been the same. Ever!

And now you too can have this (experience/results/outcome/life/money/job/relationship...) in the five easy steps described in this book...

This formula makes me gag. A lot.

Herein lies one of my major gripes with self-help. We have all heard the stories. So and so transformed their life after such and such happened. So why can't we? 'Cause it ain't that simple... And we forget that simple fact because of our never-ending hope that one day, once and for all, we really will be fixed. We hold out hope that one day we will never doubt again, we will never fear again, we will never wonder again. We will always be happy, thin, rich, successful, satisfied, smart, and spiritual. So we keep buying the books, taking the classes, studying with the masters, ad infinitum.

As I have heard in the rooms of Twelve-Step recovery: We strive for progress, not perfection. But how many of us on the self-help path say, "Oh, yes, progress is enough for me!" That is, how many would say it and actually *mean* it? Most of us—and if you're still reading this book I'm going to assume you are one of us—are waiting until we are perfect and doing everything perfectly—which will never happen.

Maybe there are people who do it perfectly, all the time. They seem to write books that say they do. I haven't met any. The people I know continue to grapple.

Shortly after the fire, a well-meaning friend told me to "snap out of it." I politely declined. I knew it was simply not time to snap out of it. I needed to be where I was in my grief. I wasn't ready to put the stamp of transformation on my experience. It wasn't time to realize all the lessons from this fire.

Then, less politely I called one of my friends with whom I could bare all and railed, "Snap out of it! What the @#*&! does that even mean?!"

She laughed at me gently and praised my anger. "Good!" she said. "You're expressing some of that pent-up anger! It's about time."

Feeling more spacious, I got to look my anger in the eye. Angry? Why yes, I believe I was.

We then talked about my chronic need to be good and nice; to do the right thing; to always use my spiritual tool kit; to create an empowering context. And, again, I am not knocking all that—but all you "good spiritual folks" out there know what I mean. You know just how disempowering it can get when you don't have permission to access the full range of your emotions—when some emotions are deemed more legitimate and valid than others.

Many of us become trapped in the persona of perfection. I have so many years of personal development under my belt that I am habituated to look for the gift. Again, nothing wrong here, except that I may skip over some of the ugly. My client and friend Sara Nowlin is writing a book called *Loving Your Ugly*—a title I resonate with deeply. She explores how easy it is to say that we will love all parts of ourselves—and how very difficult, in fact, it is to do that.

For years, I have preached the "embrace your humanity" theme. I have always appreciated rawness, realness and deep feelings. And after the fire a deeper awareness came of how I didn't really accept all my messiness and muck.

There is a trap that many of us who are on a transformational journey fall into. We think that because we "know" better we should always "be" better. And, thus we don't allow much space to allow for angst and upset.

This transformational perfection is exhausting. We are not supposed to be cheerleaders always. "Create something new—woo-hoo." "See what lie you are telling yourself—oh my." "Just what are you attracting in to your life—gag me"… It can become too much. We also can fall into the trap of "transformation-speak," where every word that comes out of our mouths sounds like jargon. I have been guilty of this myself—after two decades of being on the "path," I have been thoroughly indoctrinated. I speak recovery, I speak therapist, I speak transformation, and I speak spirituality. Particular phrases and words are used for a reason within each of these areas. They capture a mood, an essence, a message, and communicate it clearly to those of us who need our B.S. penetrated deeply. But to the uninitiated, they can be off-putting. And sometimes, even to the initiated, they can be off-putting!

I am not saying I won't use lingo—I am suggesting that those of us who use the lingo need to be aware of how it might affect another person. Do you know how hard it was to write that previous sentence without all sorts of lingo to express my call for less lingo??? Quite hard.

The real point is, let's not hide behind lingo. Let's not slap a label on stuff. I am not disempowered, I am grieving. It's not that I am not willing to create what's possible, I am simply letting myself mourn. I needed to be just where I was, messy humanity, tears, snot, heartbreak, and all. The permission to be ourselves comes from within. What keeps us waiting to grant that permission is fear—fear of the unknown, fear we might break down for good and not come back, fear of not being accepted, etc. When we give ourselves permission, we grant ourselves freedom to be. At this point, our emotions can do a lot of great work if we stop interfering with their job. Tears can soften us into love or laughter when we allow them to flow, slow, and complete, instead of choking them back. Anger can help us set a good boundary and remind us of our power to say what's so for us. These two emotions—sadness and anger—get a bad rap in our Ever-Sunny American culture, but their healthy expression is not what's damaging. What's damaging is when we suppress them so viciously that they tend to explode, dominate, and stick around way too long, just like moody teenagers locked in a basement without food or iPods.

I want to thank my friend who helped me clarify for myself where I was and where I needed to be—she knows who she is.

Throughout this book, I have been sharing my dedication to let myself be where I am in my process. I do this for myself (of course) and also for those out there who crave the permission to let themselves be. Funny that the permission we seek to be ourselves ultimately comes from within. We are our own jail-keepers, but we keep pressing or rebelling against some invisible force out there somewhere or deep down somewhere and keep the bars intact. That is just plain silly, isn't it? I am not saying we don't have external pressures and voices that assist in our staying stuck, but really, in the end, it all comes down to us. Most of us know this intellectually, but living it is a totally different ballgame.

Gentle Knock:

Where are you hiding behind the persona of perfection? Where are you uncomfortable with your own messiness? Do you think that because you have the tools, that means you are always supposed to use them?

What about expanding your tool kit to include allowing some disallowed emotions? What do you think might happen if you were to experiment (consciously) with anger, fear, or sadness?

Susan, an aspiring author and workshop leader, told me this story:

> *I was introduced to one of the big gurus when I was very young. Growing up in an environment where we only talked about the positive was amazing. I learned tools and steps and processes to manifest what I wanted. If something didn't happen for me, I was clear that*

either I didn't really want it or that somehow I had let one of my "unfriendly" ways of thinking slip out. We worked endlessly on vanquishing our old and destructive thought patterns. We visualized them slipping away with the tide, or disappearing in a puff of smoke or even being buried in the earth. After these sessions, I always felt lighter and easier. I smiled often, I had many friends, I succeeded at my work, and I attracted wonderful men into my life.

Then one day, a member of my program told us about a horrific event that had happened to her daughter. The crowd hushed as she shared her tears and anger. The leader stopped her mid-sentence and said, "Don't speak those words, you will only attract more of it. You need to realize that on some level your daughter attracted that in her life—and you need to consider that you did too." I felt a ripple run through the crowd. Some people seemed to be shaking their heads in agreement; others seemed as shocked as I felt. Yes, I could understand in theory what was being said—yet here was this woman who was clearly grief-stricken, and she was being shut down—and dare I say blamed? I was outraged, yet I knew if I opened my mouth at that moment, I would be "coached" as well. That night I tossed and turned. I thought of all the great things that had happened in my life. I loved feeling positive and attracting more positive experiences. And I had often questioned how to reconcile it when "negative" things happened.

I always believed we could (and would) learn from any event if we were open. But still, as I saw in this woman's eyes, I knew great pain existed in the world, and I wanted to make room for that too. Over the next few months, I came to my own realization, which felt like a new level of growing up. I left the guru and the program on good terms, truly grateful for all I had learned, but ready to allow myself—and others—to feel the bigger range of human experiences, without needing to censor raw emotions. To tell you the truth, by letting myself feel my unhappiness, I feel happier than ever before.

Yes, there are great teachers and great lessons to learn. There are great books to read and great courses to take. We will gain insight and knowledge and will even take on new behaviors. The field of self-help that has fed me for so many years is both an ally and a nemesis. It promises that the next hot thing—the perfect question, the perfect mantra, the perfect inquiry, and the perfect ritual—will be the thing that will make everything fall into place. I don't know about you, but I have been attempting to have everything fall into place for a very long time. And, when I look around, it's not in place. Not at all. Not much is where it should be or how I think it should be. And, if it is in place for a moment, it falls out seconds later.

This is not to say that massive overhauls such as getting sober don't alter us. I am not the lost little girl who binged and purged her way through life back in the '80s. Writing my first book did in fact demonstrate that I am capable of writing, and so I take that knowledge and demonstration into the writing of my second and third. But really, when you look at it, in so many ways we are really the same—just bigger, older, more wrinkled versions of our former eager selves.

Gentle Knock:

Where are you stuck on your own self-help treadmill? How have you used your tools of transformation to beat yourself up?

What parts of yourself tend to get dishonored and disregarded when you cling too tightly to an "ideal" version of who you should be?

Fire changes everything; destroying all in its unpredictable path. And fire can bond. I see the physical evidence of that in our rubble. I see it in our beautiful handmade front door with the antique stained glass lovingly crafted by my mentors, Bill and Sandy. We found clumps of twisted glass embedded in our metal doormat. The elements have come together permanently. Now part of a collection of artifacts, they have been born again with a dark beauty of their own—scarred, mangled, gnarled, yet strong and fierce. There is synthesis from the rage of the fire.

I have to assume that is happening to me too. Transformation is occurring, some of it without my conscious intention or permission. I do not yet know who I will be on the other side. I am in the proverbial hallway between what was and what will be. What will matter to me? How will I choose to spend my time once the vast amount of insurance paperwork is complete? What will my work be? What is my mission? The cloud of grief obscures what is to come. I realize I don't have to know right now. I attempt to let myself hang out in the unknown. I hope to emerge like the glass and twisted metal that survived: changed, rich in character—and not ever the same.

I am ready to discover the metaphors for fire. I seek a mystical explanation of this grand adventure. There have been plenty of signs of the mystical operating both in the background and the foreground. I am not ready to share all of it yet, but I know it's there. And, it is coming. It is part of my transformation.

The metaphors will haunt me if I don't stop and face them. This is my healing path. I continue this written exploration not knowing what is to come in my words, but needing to follow this train. I continue with an honoring heart.

Who I was is burning up. In this process, it is slower and more deliberate than the wildfire that consumed my home.

Chapter 17:

Wait No More?

I wanted a perfect ending. Now I've learned, the hard way, that some poems don't rhyme, and some stories don't have a clear beginning, middle, and end. Life is about not knowing, having to change, taking the moment and making the best of it, without knowing what's going to happen next. Delicious Ambiguity.

— GILDA RADNER

To create a sense of "home" on our burned out land, we hired a lovely man named Javier to build us a flagstone patio where we could stop and smell the roses—or attempt to not inhale the ashes, whichever the case might be. As Javier was preparing to depart, he gazed one last time at our panoramic view, the burn not registering as detraction in any way, and these words came out of his mouth, "At least you…"

Now, here's what you need to know. Ever since the fire, these words have been the prelude to a (generally) inflammatory statement, as people uncomfortable with tragedy fill in the blank with something they think we should be grateful for. "At least you have insurance." "At least you got your pets out." "At least you have good friends." I was warned by other survivors of fire that this would happen, and happen it does. This time, however, my heart opened to Javier as he finished: "…have this land and this view." I again heartily agreed with him.

Yes, at least we do have this land and this view. We are quite fortunate. We have a beautiful and serene spot, even with its most recent scars and destruction. Here is the rich fabric of life: I can realize my blessings and still have my slumps. I can be grateful for how relatively "easy" we have it compared to so many others, and I can let go of needing to experience that gratitude at every moment. I don't have to wait for that anymore.

Yesterday at my Twelve-Step meeting the topic was "letting

go," a common theme of conversation around the rooms. It's always interesting to hear the many different perspectives on this topic. Some are short and sweet; others are a long, tall order. Many parables are shared to illustrate the simplicity of letting go coupled with our innate human ability to complicate and resist anything simple. Letting go really does sound easy. And most of us know that it's not. It is simple; it is not easy. We can let go—and then a few minutes (or seconds) later, pick it right back up again. Many of us are like a ravenous dog with a bone, gnawing away until our gums bleed.

After one particularly moving share, I reconfirmed my knowledge that I will ultimately let go. I will do it, it will happen, this too shall pass, and yadda yadda. This is the big-picture view. In the small-picture view, where most of us live, I need to be where I am. It goes like this:

Let go, pick it back up, let go again... Aah, space and freedom. Trigger trigger trigger. Shit!!!!!!!!! Breathe. Let go. OK, got it. I am letting go. Peace. Wait a minute—what did you say? Spiral spiral spiral. Oh, you didn't mean "that"? You really love me? OK, I understand. I feel happy! We really are OK. What? Another wildfire is burning in our state, more people died? What's wrong with the world?

Why is there so much suffering? Wow, that is a beautiful sunset. Ooooh, did you see that baby deer? Boy, I love my dogs. Oh no, I have a sore throat, maybe I am getting sick. Shit. God does hate me. There isn't even a God anyway. Nothing makes sense. I am sleepy. I love my cozy bed. So glad to have my feather pillow. Aah. Life is good. Right now. In this moment. I hope nothing happens today...

Our busy mind, with its incessant thoughts, is our constant companion. The Buddhists call it the Monkey Mind: Capricious, restless, easily distracted, it screams its chatter into our vulnerable ears. As it clamors for attention, some have an easier time keeping it locked in its cage and remembering that it tells us a pack of lies. Others have what we call in Twelve-Step rooms a "built-in forgetter." In 1989, I learned this simplest of explanations for my seemingly crazy thoughts: I simply forget my fear isn't the truth. I forget over and over and over and over again. And then I remember, when I remember. Sometimes, I remember more quickly, sometimes it takes me a while. With a long-term dedication to a path of personal growth comes the experience of having walked through many fires in our lives. Once we walk through enough fires, we begin to know on some higher level that, one day, we will be OK again. And one day, we will see the gifts. And one day, the event will recede into the distance, becoming part of our history but not informing everything we think, say, or do.

Why should we resist our wild and wacky human nature? Most of us self-helpers and spiritual seekers have heard that "what you resist persists." When we are opposed to something, we put our attention on our opposition and we actually strengthen it, harden it, and calcify it into something concrete that becomes "just the way it is"—whatever "it" might be.

What if we weren't opposed to anything—especially our own human foibles? What if we accepted Gandhi's well-publicized invitation to *be* the change we want to *see* and actually started with ourselves, regardless of our circumstances?

One of the most important things I am letting go of today is how "letting go" itself should look. For this human, letting go is a process, not a one-time event. I am like the weather— sometimes sunny, sometimes cloudy. Sometimes blowing stink, sometimes pitter-pattering cool drops of rain. I will open my heart to people like Javier and allow myself to view my world through his kind eyes. And sometimes I will wake up grumpy and argue with my husband for no apparent reason. Then I will back up and remember that he is my favorite person in the whole wide world and all I really want is for him to be happy. And then I will pat his head, offer more coffee, and make my amends. Later, I may moan and groan on hold at customer service. I will pat my dogs and be gratefully elated at their presence. I will celebrate the small amount of "old" things I carried out of my house, like my wool turtleneck sweater and handwoven blanket.

We will forget, then we will remember, then we will forget again. And, one day, we will remember longer.

Recently, I found a piece I wrote on March 24—a mere two days before the fire:

Life

If we had known, would we have taken this journey? If we had known we would forget who we are, spend much of our lives being our worst enemy, run ourselves into the ground only to one day realize that nothing really matters except love—would we have said yes to this adventure?

They say wisdom comes with age—and we know that that is not a guaranteed outcome. It takes a willingness to become self-aware, which is distinct from being self-conscious. Self-awareness is having perspective on ourselves as well as on our silly human foibles without making any of it wrong—or catching ourselves as soon as we begin to make it wrong. Self-consciousness is extreme self-absorption, which is not wrong either; it's just a distraction from who we really are.

I celebrated arriving to my forties as I heard that the forties are an age when one begins to be less concerned with all the things that seemed so important before. The hope was a mellowing of the need to be liked, a softening of my driven-ness, and a deeper level of self-acceptance. I believe it has been. And now, as I turn the corner on my mid-forties, heading down the next stretch, toward my fifties, I take stock again of where I am and who I have become.

These thoughts remained an unfinished exploration, sitting on my computer, waiting for a conclusion. I don't have one now.

Instead, I wonder who I will become on the other side of this grand adventure. My world rocked the day my house burned to the ground. Life, as I knew it altered, and everything changed. I realize I don't need to know why it happened. I do want to know that I will grow. I am not who I was on that day, and I still don't quite know who I will be. Not that I was all that bad before, but guess what? You'll never believe it, but

I want transformation from this. I want to be deeper, stronger, and wiser on the other side. I want to be more willing to let go and to dance in the unknown.

Who knows what the future will hold? I certainly hope that we may have smooth waters for a bit. But just because this happened, it doesn't mean that won't. We need to buckle our seatbelts for this wild ride called life. I can choose to let go of my white-knuckled grip on the armrests and actually look out the window.

I am able to dance on the brink of the abyss because, deep down in my bones, I know I will be OK. And the knowing doesn't mean I always know. There are many moments when I forget. Yet the knowing remains. I return to it. It's a quiet voice, or simply a sensation. It's an experience of freedom. I now know I can and will walk through anything. Please don't test me on that, though! I am certainly not asking for any more fabulous life lessons for the near future. This morning, I was mourning. I missed my home and some of my life before the fire. Then, I rolled over in bed and looked first at my sleeping dogs, one at my feet and the other curled up on his bed. Then I looked at David. "Aah," I sighed. "These creatures are all that really matter."

Gentle Knock:

We've all experienced situations in our lives or in the world around us that have served as a reminder to wake up in some way—or to remember what really matters to us. When this happens, how do you relate to that wake-up call over time, as life moves on? Do you continue to stay awake or do you hit the snooze button and go back to sleep? What is one area of your life where you've hit the snooze button on your wake-up call, and what will it take for you to go for it? What is it that *really* matters to you? Look at your waiting and try to see where it is gentle, compassionate, honoring a process, and where it simply serves to keep you stuck exactly where you are.

This thing called life is just life. It's just what happens and how we react. The ground will continue to move under our feet. We count on the sun rising each morning and the day being similar to the day before. We have to count on that; otherwise, we would lose our center. Yet down deep we know we can't count on anything. It's all up for grabs as we spin through space in a universe we can barely grasp, in a world that might not ever make sense, until it does.

Rains come and wash away the first layers of soot on our land. But it is so deep, so thick, it seems that it goes on forever. It seems nothing can take the blackness away. It will never return to what it once was. Later, a layer of snow falls, covering the blackness. Suddenly, it looks different. The destruction is blanketed in white. I know that it is still there, yet for a moment it remains out of view. The snow melts and reveals the blackness—but is that blackness any lighter? A few green sprouts emerge from the ground. Are they hope? Will they make it? They are so small it seems they can't ever make a difference.

It rains again. Some of the smell dissipates. I only catch wafts of it now, traces of burn. Or is it that I am getting accustomed to the new fragrance?

Groups of angels in human form descend and begin to pick up the pieces. Slowly, surely, steadily, the rubble is removed. Treasures emerge from the mess—little signs of something.

Reminders of a life lived. Reminders of love given and received.

Ah, I remember: All we have is now, everything is OK. We humans can realize we are whole, complete, and perfect—and, in the next moment we forget all of this. Then in a moment we forget, and we can remember again.

The site continues to be transformed. I don't know what it will be. I don't know who I will be. I don't know who I am. Yet I do know. I am a Phoenix emerging from the fire.

Now I wait no longer, until I wait again.

And I am restored to wonder.

Final Words

Doesn't everything die at last, and too soon?
Tell me, what is it you plan to do
with your one wild and precious life?
—MARY OLIVER, "THE SUMMER
DAY"

I t's a good day to die," I said to my seatmate as our plane ascended into the heavens. Not my usual opening line but one I felt strongly about in the moment. I knew the next day might be a different story, as normally, I am not a big fan of dying.

With the anniversary of the fire approaching, and of my yearlong journey through grief, I chose to partake in a transformational weekend with my trusted coach. Always walking that fine line between finding my own truth and bouncing things off my mentors, I decided a weekend immersion in the themes, blocks, gifts, and lessons of the year prior was just what I needed. Add in the bonus that this particular coach was the one who spoke wise and necessary words to my fire-ravaged heart in those early days, "Don't come too quickly to form," she said. As you have seen in these pages, I took her words to heart. Instead of "coming to form," I let myself have my grief—the big, the messy, the snotty, and the beautiful.

Yet, even though I committed to this weekend of coaching and knew it would be transformational, I began to wonder months before if it really was the right time. Did I really feel up to this work? Did I even want to go? Maybe, just maybe, if I waited a little bit longer I might feel more ready.

My grief had lifted in many ways, yet the dark circles under my eyes and a chronic feeling of fatigue remained. A lightness had returned to my step and a new view of life had begun to emerge, yet perhaps if I waited until after the anniversary of the fire… or after my vacation… or after something… it might be better.

Later, is what I thought. Perhaps, later.

Yet as with any very good coach, my plea for later was a

"no go." This was an agreement we had made. It was in our schedules. It was to be now, or not at all.

So I found myself in California with my coach, with the plan to symbolically complete my year of transformation that began with the fire. As we looked at where I had been and where I was going, the challenges began: "What is it that blocks you? What is it that still stands in your way? Will you fully be yourself and bare your essence now, or will you hide? Will you do it halfway or will you play full out?"

These weren't her exact words, but the sentiment penetrated deeply. She bore in and backed off, then bore in again. She made space, then held me tight, and then told me she was there to catch me when I faltered.

I cast about for what held me back. I sought the answer to the ever-elusive question of why I wait—and what it would take in *that instant* to stop waiting.

After many tears, much laughter, bold action, baring my soul, and some gorgeous moments, I felt lighter than I have in years. And, as I checked out of my hotel room to begin my journey home, the lurking feeling that I was leaving something behind kept popping up. It happened again as I left the restaurant where I had breakfast, and then again as I got out of my friend's car at the airport. As I hunted for what it might be, I realized what it was. I was leaving behind a part of me.

Goethe's words express the thoughts that flooded my mind

as I boarded my flight home: "Our passions are the true phoenixes; when the old one is burnt out, a new one rises from its ashes."

In the time it took me to fly back home, perhaps you have finished reading this book. As you re-emerge from these pages, you may have noticed that the world hasn't stopped, slowed, or even changed that much. So what has changed?

In our journey together, we peered into the nooks and crannies of life. We shone light into dusty and musty corners, and swept out the cobwebs. We looked at the major areas we wait, that drag us down into the muck, as well as the subtle yet just as debilitating ones. We distinguished between when it's wise to wait versus being "doers" who burn ourselves into the ground. We talked about moving forward when every molecule screams *stop*.

We realized that life is unpredictable, that it has many ups and downs and will continue to "life us." We learned we can be OK with that, even when we are not feeling OK.

And we admitted we will forget everything, including just how fabulous we are, and then we will remember again.

I bared my darkness and shared my pain. You heard from others who had an epiphany that in turn altered their path in life.

Through the "gentle knocks" I offered, you have been able to take your own journey and tell yourself (and hopefully a few trusted others) your truth—your dark secrets and your bright joys.

I pray you had new insights along the way. Perhaps my words have rekindled lost or hidden dreams. Perhaps old fears have awakened, and stumbling blocks seem to be in your way. You may be flying high, coasting low, or in a downswing. At the very least, I hope you have illuminated the subtle or not so subtle ways you wait.

And what now?

You could simply turn this page, walk away, and be done.

Now it's up to you. As always, the transformation part is up to you. What you do from here on is your choice.

Yes, I left something in my hotel and in the restaurant and in my friend's car. As I sat gazing out the airplane window then, I uttered those words to my stunned seatmate, I felt more complete than ever before. In that moment, I realized that it's all just moments. Life is a string of moments. That's all. In one moment I gave up waiting, and in another moment, I might wait again.

Yet we string together a bunch of these moments when we refuse to wait, and as a result we have something that resembles grace. Grace is what I felt on the plane. Grace and presence and beauty—and all those indescribable emotions that make being human so damned amazing. In that moment of grace, had I accomplished everything in this life that I set out to accomplish? No. But I knew I had pushed my limits, lived deeply, loved extraordinarily—and in that weekend with my coach I had left behind another small piece of what holds me back.

Will it return? Who knows? But right now, I am complete. I die to my old way of being. I die to my fear. I die to my grief.

Do I want to die really? No, I want to live. But in order for us to stop waiting, we have to let part of us die off. To do that, we must do what scares us, then rest when we need to rest, and then do what scares us again.

What will you do with it? Will you live that dream, take that plunge, step that baby step, or leap that leap? Will you fold at the slightest sign of a roadblock? Will you whisper on your deathbed that you wish you had lived differently?

What will you do with your one wild precious life?

ABOUT THE AUTHOR

After losing her dream home and all her worldly possessions to a raging and sudden wildfire that killed three
people and demolished twenty-one homes, Kristen
Moeller dove headfirst into an exploration of our cultural
discomfort with grief, the existence of God, finding humor in
the midst of tragedy—and what it means to be a human being
with all our fabulousness as well as frailties.

In her writing, Kristen draws on a rich life experience, professional training as a therapist and coach, deep spiritual beliefs,
double-decade recovery from addiction, and her twisted, dark
humor. In the early '90s Kristen earned a master's degree in
counseling psychology and counseled individuals and groups in
the fields of addiction and personal growth. After writing her
first book in 2008, Kristen found true passion in helping other
authors find their voice as writers.

Once viewed as "shy," Kristen can now be found in venues

as diverse as TEDx stages, stand-up comedy clubs, and her own radio show (aptly called "What Are You Waiting For?"), as well as appearances on local TV and national radio. In all mediums, Kristen lives her commitment to share her wisdom, yet readily admits that, even after years of self-growth, the twists and turns of life can still throw her.

As part of her fierce commitment to helping others find their own path to personal freedom, Kristen founded the TransformationFoundation.org which provides "pay-it-forward" scholarships for transformational education programs worldwide.

When relaxing, she divides her time between a yurt in the mountains of Colorado, cruising the open road in her 1960 Airstream trailer, and sailing in the Bahamas.

For more information about Kristen, please visit: www.kristenmoeller.com

Photograph by Christina Morassi.

To Our Readers

Viva Editions publishes books that inform, enlighten, and entertain. We do our best to bring you, the reader, quality books that celebrate life, inspire the mind, revive the spirit, and enhance lives all around. Our authors are practical visionaries: people who offer deep wisdom in a hopeful and helpful manner. Viva was launched with an attitude of growth and we want to spread our joy and offer our support and advice where we can to help you live the Viva way: vivaciously!

We're grateful for all our readers and want to keep bringing you books for inspired living. We invite you to write to us with your comments and suggestions, and what you'd like to see more of. You can also sign up for our online newsletter to learn about new titles, author events, and special offers.

Viva Editions
2246 Sixth St.
Berkeley, CA 94710
www.vivaeditions.com
(800) 780-2279
Follow us on Twitter @vivaeditions
Friend/fan us on Facebook